Philosophy of Finitude

Also available from Bloomsbury

Desire in Ashes: Deconstruction, Psychoanalysis, Philosophy, edited by Chiara Alfano and Simon Morgan Wortham
Heidegger and the Emergence of the Question of Being, Jesús Adrián Escudero
Heidegger, History and the Holocaust, Mahon O'Brien
Heidegger and Nietzsche, Louis P. Blond
Between Levinas and Lacan, Mari Ruti
Lacan Contra Foucault: Subjectivity, Sex, and Politics, edited by Nadia Bou Ali and Rohit Goel
Foucault and Nietzsche, edited by Alan Rosenberg and Joseph Westfall
Nietzsche and Political Thought, edited by Keith Ansell-Pearson

Philosophy of Finitude

Heidegger, Levinas and Nietzsche

Rafael Winkler

BLOOMSBURY ACADEMIC
LONDON • NEW YORK • OXFORD • NEW DELHI • SYDNEY

BLOOMSBURY ACADEMIC
Bloomsbury Publishing Plc
50 Bedford Square, London, WC1B 3DP, UK
1385 Broadway, New York, NY 10018, USA

BLOOMSBURY, BLOOMSBURY ACADEMIC and the Diana logo are trademarks of
Bloomsbury Publishing Plc

First published in Great Britain 2018

Cover design: Irene Martinez-Costa
Cover image © Time House / Alamy Stock Photo

A catalogue record for this book is available from the British Library.

A catalog record for this book is available from the Library of Congress.

ISBN: HB: 978-1-3500-5936-8
ePDF: 978-1-3500-5935-1
ePub: 978-1-3500-5937-5

Typeset by Newgen KnowledgeWorks Pvt. Ltd., Chennai, India

To find out more about our authors and books visit www.bloomsbury.com
and sign up for our newsletters.

To Mira and Salomé,
And to the memory of my mother

Contents

Acknowledgements

I owe an infinite debt of gratitude to a good number of people who have seen this project through, both in part and as a whole, since its inception in the winter of 2015 at a retreat in a lodge in Magaliesburg, South Africa. These include: Babette Babich, Dan Dahlstrom, Joanna Hodge, Ulli Haase, Dermot Moran, Paul Patton, John Sallis and Miguel de Beistegui. I owe a special thanks to Thad Metz who generously offered to organize a reading group on an early draft of the book. A thanks is also due to the participants whose contribution improved the book a thousandfold: Jaco Kruger, Gary Beck, Jimmy Kyriacou, Marquard Dirk Pienaar, David Martens, Anton van Niekerk, Pete Wolfendale, and David Mitchell. I also owe thanks to my parents, Jean-Pierre Winkler and Simone Hellebosch, for their continued support.

Lastly, I would like to thank my partner, Katlego, and my daughters, Salomé and Mira, for having seen me through the completion of this project. Life has, since I have known them, become light, a dance and a joy.

Abbreviations

Heidegger's works:

BP   *The Basic Problems of Phenomenology*. Trans. Albert Hofstadter.
      Bloomington and Indianapolis: Indiana University Press, 1982

BT   *Being and Time*. Trans. John Macquarrie and Edward Robinson.
      Oxford, UK and Cambridge, MA: Blackwell, 1991

BW   *Basic Writings*. Ed. David Farrell Krell. New York: HarperCollins, 1993

CP   *Contributions to Philosophy (Of the Event)*. Trans. Richard Rojcewicz
      and Daniela Vallega-Nue. Bloomington and Indianapolis: Indiana
      University Press, 2012

DT   *Discourse on Thinking*. Trans. John M. Anderson and E. Hans Freund.
      New York: Harper & Row, 1966

EGT   *Early Greek Thinking*. Trans. David Farrell Krell and Frank A. Capuzzi.
      New York: Harper & Row, 1984

EHP   *Elucidations of Hölderlin's Poetry*. Trans. Keith Hoeller. New York:
      Humanity Books, 2000

HCT   *History of the Concept of Time. Prolegomena*. Trans. Theodore Kisiel.
      Bloomington and Indianapolis: Indiana University Press, 1992

HGR   *Hölderlin's Hymns 'Germania' and 'The Rhine'*. Trans. William McNeill
      and Julia Ireland. Bloomington and Indianapolis: Indiana University
      Press, 2014

HH   *Hölderlin's Hymn 'The Ister'*. Trans. William McNeill and Julia Davis.
      Bloomington and Indianapolis: Indiana University Press, 1996

MFL   *The Metaphysical Foundations of Logic*. Trans. Michael Heim.
      Bloomington and Indianapolis: Indiana University Press, 1992

N1–4 *Nietzsche, 4 vols*. Trans. David Farrell Krell. New York:
      HarperCollins, 1991

OBT   *Off the Beaten Track*. Ed. and Trans. Julian Young and Kenneth Haynes. Cambridge, UK: Cambridge University Press, 2002

P   *Parmenides*. Trans. André Schuwer and Richard Rojcewicz. Bloomington and Indianapolis: Indiana University Press, 1998

PLT   *Poetry, Language, Thought*. Trans. Albert Hofstadter. New York: Harper & Row, 1971)

PM   *Pathmarks*. Ed. William McNeill, 1998

PRL   *The Phenomenology of Religious Life*. Trans. Matthias Fritsch and Jennifer Anna Gossetti-Ferencei. Bloomington and Indianapolis: Indiana University Press, 2010

PR   *The Principle of Reason*. Trans. Reginald Lilly. Bloomington and Indianapolis: Indiana University Press, 1991

TDP   *Towards the Definition of Philosophy*. Trans. Ted Sadler. London and New York: Continuum, 2000

WCT   *What is Called Thinking?* Trans. Fred D. Wieck and J. Glenn Gray. New York, Evanston, and London: Harper & Row, Publishers, 1968

Zo   *Zollikon Seminars: Protocols – Conversations – Letters*. Ed. Medard Boss. Trans. Franz Mayr and Richard Askay. Evanston, IL: Northwestern University Press, 2001

Introduction

This book attempts to justify, perhaps not always very successfully, the belief that the unique is everything or, to put it more precisely using one of Plato's expressions, that the unique is *to ontos on, the really real*.

By *the unique* I do not mean that which responds to the question *who are you?*, that is, the first person whose identity constitutes itself as it narrates its life to the other.

The dominant theory of experience from Descartes to Husserl, including Kant, either conflates the uniqueness of experience with the first person or it accounts for the former by reference to the latter. A Kantian or a phenomenologist, the difference does not matter in this regard, will say that my perception of the red cube is incommensurable with yours because that first perception is *mine*.

I argue in Chapter 1 of this book that uniqueness is prior in meaning to and that it makes possible the constitution of the first person. An experience can be unique and anonymous at the same time, that is to say, it can be left unclaimed by the self.

That is especially true in the case of limit experiences or traumas of different sorts where someone suffers the complete collapse of their personal identity. The sense of that person's life grows dark. She is no longer capable of referring to herself as *I*. Nevertheless, that does not mean that her experience has become qualitatively indistinguishable from someone else's whose personal identity has also broken down. As I put it in this book, a life is and remains non-replaceable, singular or unique, even when the unity of the first person has broken down, and it is no longer possible to think in the first person or ascribe experiences to the *I*.

To justify that position, I argue in Chapter 1 against transcendental philosophy's claim that the collapse of the unity of the first person is not a possible experience. Drawing on cases of schizophrenia in Ronald Laing's *The Divided Self* and Heidegger's description of anxiety in *What is Metaphysics?*, I show that the collapse of the unity of the self is a possible experience and that possible experience, consequently, does not depend on the unity of the first person as a necessary condition of possibility.

What accounts for the non-replaceability of a life if not the unity of the first person? *Uniqueness* is not a feature that descends from heaven (the immortality of the person). Or at least I don't believe that it does.

Like the word *being*, uniqueness is not a predicate with an empirical or eidetic content. It does not pick out an accidental property or essence. It tells us nothing about who or what one is. *Uniqueness* is not the essence of the human being. It is a purely formal feature of existence. One is non-replaceable just by virtue of existing (that is, of being to the measure of Dasein).

Consequently, the haecceity of a being, that is, someone's *thisness* or uniqueness, is not determined by a numerical or material difference, as is generally believed in the Aristotelian tradition (one's position in space and time; the hue of one's skin or hair, the molecular structure of one's body; one's habits or dispositions or, more generally, one's character). Rather, if *uniqueness* is a formal feature of existence, then it must be determined by a difference that is equally formal and unique.

There are, in that regard, at least two possible candidates for that difference or principle of singularization. There is the imminence of death, according to Heidegger, and there is the responsibility for the other, according to Ricoeur and Levinas.

Irrespective of whether the first or the second has a priority of meaning (which, besides, I am not sure that it is possible to decide), in both of these cases, we are thinking of a life in its singularity in distinction from the numerical identity of a person or that of a substance and of the taxonomic apparatus that pertains to the latter (genus, species, specific difference), as Porphyry sets it out in his *Isagoge*.

Generally speaking, my aim in this book is to demonstrate that it is necessary to take thought beyond the limits imposed by the concept, language and experience of identity in order to be faithful, as far as possible, to the thought of uniqueness. A thinking of uniqueness is a thinking of absolute difference, and that calls for a thinking of finitude.

Let me explain. I can view myself from the first or from the third person standpoint, that is, as a person (*who*) or as a thing (*what*). I usually tend to do both in my unreflective and sometimes in my reflective engagement with others in the world. I often identify with others on the basis of shared experiences. I also identify with them on the basis of the fact that we have the same job or the same gender or because we are part of the same race, religion or nationality, etc.

At least two things follow from this kind of constitution of personal and social identity. To have an identity is to be a member of some groups and to be excluded from others. As feminist scholars and political theorists have been emphasizing in the last few decades, an identity is a norm and standard of inclusion and exclusion that creates insiders and outsiders (see Butler 1990, Edkins 2007, Perpich 2010, Winkler 2016).

In the second place, and as Heidegger tells us in his discussion of the inauthenticity of Dasein in *Being and Time*, if I regard myself in terms of what I do, then I inevitably see myself as someone who is replaceable by others. I am a teacher (say) and, as such, I am replaceable by any other teacher. It is no different when I identify with others on the basis of shared experiences or third personal characteristics. I claim ownership of my existence in these social roles, shared experiences, or through these third personal characteristics as something that is common and, therefore, exchangeable with others.

To be unique, on the other hand, is to be unlike any other. It is to be, like an absolute origin, without precedent in history or nature. The unique is beyond the distinction between *insider* and *outsider*. It is the absolutely other. Or what amounts to the same thing, it is the without-identity, the anonymous or the absolute stranger.

The unique marks the finitude of language and thought. That is not because it is ineffable. It is said that the individual is ineffable (*individuum est ineffabile*). That is because the notion of an individual substance has an infinite intension (and, correlatively, an extension that is equal to 1) that only God's infinite intellect can comprehend. For example, Leibniz claims that a contingent being is grasped in its *thisness* by adding together the infinite number of predicates that are true of it in its 'complete individual concept'.

But the unique is not the individual, as I argue in Chapter 1. Besides, an existent is manifest in its uniqueness not when all the predicates that are true of it have been added to its notion but once it has been deprived of all the characteristics that it could have in common with others, that is, once it has been stripped of *all* conceivable characteristics (since there is no characteristic that an existent has that could not be instantiated by another). When nothing more can be said of it except *that it is*, then and only then does it stand apart and shine through in the singularity of its existence.

Put differently, an existent stands out in its absolute non-replaceability when thought confronts the absolute impossibility of classifying it under taxonomic systems in general, of determining it under the concept of an object, or of identifying it under the categories of being such as *thing-property* and, more broadly even, under the modern distinction between *thing* and *person*, *something* and *someone*, *what* and *who*.

The unique is, strictly speaking, the unclassifiable, the unidentifiable. That is why an experience of it (providing that an experience of it is possible, which is not at all certain, if it is true that the possibility of experience involves the possibility of identification, of determination under a concept, of the institution of equivalents and of their substitution, of the symbolic exchangeability of a being by an instance of the same or of another kind, of the reproduction of the present in a representation, etc.) leaves us speechless, is traumatic, is, like an event that cannot be anticipated in advance, an absolute surprise, a shock. It brings thought back before the absolute impossibility of thought, or the limit of the thinkable. Again not because it is ineffable but, rather, because it is without a determinable identity. The content of the unique is determined by nothing save alterity and strangeness, the strangeness of *being there at all*. The thinking of the unique is a thinking of finitude.

I show in Chapter 3 that this is especially evident when we think of being in Heidegger's sense of that term. *Being* in Heidegger signifies the intelligibility of entities. It denotes the way they appear, their manifestation or disclosure, their becoming-apparent to Dasein.

The intelligibility of entities in Heidegger is localized neither in a transcendental subject (transcendental idealism) nor in the entities themselves (metaphysical realism). At least that is true of Heidegger during the 1930s and 1940s. He leans towards transcendental idealism during the 1920s, identifying the intelligibility of entities (their being) with Dasein's understanding of being. During the 1930s and 1940s, Heidegger thinks of the relation of being and Dasein as a relation of reciprocal implication or mutual dependency (*belonging* and *need* are his two key terms, the first for Dasein's relation to being, the second for being's relation to Dasein), which means that he does not collapse one into the other. Being, the intelligibility of entities, unfolds as a play of differences and contrasts (*Aus-einander-setzung*), whereas Dasein shelters that play in beings (at least as long as it exists authentically).

The light (*Lichtung*) that suddenly breaks into entities articulates them in their outline and contours. It detaches them from the undifferentiated background with which they were initially fused and brings them out in relief against each other. But that light is not, in turn, an entity. It has no figure or motion or extent or mental properties. It has none of the features by which entities are usually identified, described or explained.

That is why exposure to that light, providing that were possible, would be tantamount to an exposure to nothingness, anxiety, loss of orientation, loss of self. That is perhaps why that light is also self-veiling, namely, so that Dasein can talk and engage with others in the world.

Heidegger says at the start of *Being and Time* that '*Being is the transcendens pure and simple*' and that the transcendence of Dasein's being implies 'the possibility and the necessity of the most radical *singularization*' (*BT* 62). I explain the second clause in Chapter 1. What Heidegger means to emphasize in the first clause, it seems, is the ontico-ontological difference. Being is not an entity. It is entirely other than, or it is incommensurable with, the totality of entities. We can put this by saying that *being* and *singularity* are semantically convertible terms, or that being is (none other than) singularity. It is (the) absolutely other.

What escapes the logic of the concept, the system, or identification is not only the singularity of the self (Kierkegaard) or that of the other human being (Levinas). It is, first and foremost, being as singularity.

I argue in Chapter 3 that being in that sense is unthinkable except as a figuration of someone or something or, more precisely, as a figure in which the force of the distinction between the *someone* and the *something*, the *who* and the *what*, has been suspended – as a figure, therefore, that is without a determinable identity. I argue that the feminine in Levinas and the absolute *arrivant* in Derrida are figurations of being in that sense.

In Chapter 6, I argue that what makes possible the appearance of *substantia* as a technical or ontological term in the language of the Romans is a play of metaphors and that the expressions *figure* and *metaphor* in this context cannot be used in their ordinary sense as a sensuous image that conveys a non-sensuous meaning. That is because such figures of being first articulate and make intelligible the distinction and opposition between the sensuous and the non-sensuous.

Given what *the unique* stands for – notably, something that is absolutely unlike anything that was, is, and will be present – it follows that the unique is not reducible to a context of interpretation (and that it is manifest precisely as such). It transcends history as the space and limit of hermeneutical understanding. At any rate, that is true inasmuch as to contextualize something involves tracing similarities or commonalities between it and other things past and present and situating them in a shared horizon of meaning. If we can adapt what Levinas (1979: 23) says of the other human being in *Totality and Infinity*, we can say that the unique is a signification without context.

By the same token, it also transcends the temporality of consciousness. The latter privileges the present (or, correlatively, primal impression and, in a different register, the intuitively evident) as the origin of the meaning of things, whereas the unique signifies, like a trauma, a past that was never present or a future that will never be present.

In other words, the mode of presence of the unique is the *already there* or the *to come*. It is manifest as an *originary* (or non-derivable) absence in the world. It eludes the present and, by implication, the classical sense of being as presence, at any rate, if it is true that being has since the Classical Age of the Greeks been understood by reference to the present, as both Heidegger and Levinas maintain.

I argue in the first four chapters of the book that the relation with the unique is accomplished as time, and that that is a relation, beyond consciousness and history, to an absolute past or future. That relationship takes several forms in the book, including mourning and anticipation, as well as hospitality, responsibility, dwelling and guest friendship.

This book, then, deals with the unique in a variety of ways, as the uniqueness of being, of the self, of the other human being, of death, and of the responsibility for the other. It also considers whether the unique is a possible experience and how to think and talk about it.

Chapter 1 focuses on the uniqueness of existence. I argue that the latter does not issue from the unity of the first person but from the imminence of death or the responsibility for the other. I argue in Chapter 2 that the uniqueness (or alterity) of the self does not give access to the uniqueness (or alterity) of the other human being. In Chapter 3, I argue that the uniqueness of being is unthinkable except as a figure that lacks a determinable identity and that such a figuration of being is one of the conditions necessary for something to qualify as an event or origin of meaning.

In Chapter 4, I consider some of the figurations of being that appear in Heidegger's reading of Hölderlin's lectures, starting with his 1934–5 lecture on *Germania* to his final lecture on *Der Ister* in 1942. In Chapter 5, I offer an alternative reading of Nietzsche to the one Heidegger and Derrida respectively provide and consider the non-metaphysical sense of being as light that is operative in Nietzsche's text. In the final chapter, I show that *substantia* appears as a word for being in the language and thought of the Romans through a play of metaphors, and consider the way in which such terms as *figure* and *metaphor* should be taken when what is at stake is being understood as the light that articulates the intelligibility of what there is.

This book on uniqueness would have benefitted from an engagement with the recent work of Adriana Cavarero as well as Jean-Luc Nancy's work on singularity and community. However, limitations of space and time did not allow for it. An engagement with both authors (and others) is planned in the sequel to this book.

1

Death, the Impossible

I have nothing of which I may say that it is mine.
—Friedrich Hölderlin (2011), *Hyperion*

I cannot say I.
—Paul de Man (1996), *Aesthetic Ideology*

The impossible must be done. The event, if there is one, consists in doing the impossible.
—Jacques Derrida (2007), *A Certain Impossible Possibility of Saying the Event*

1. Introduction[1]

In this chapter, I argue that the relation to death dissolves the unity of the self and that this has two serious consequences for the existential analytic of *Being and Time*. The first consequence is that a first-person ownership of the relation to death is impossible. The second consequence, which is a corollary of the first, is that a first-person ownership of one's existence before death is impossible. If I cannot own the relation to death authentically, then I cannot own my existence authentically, since the former is a necessary condition of possibility of the latter.

This does not mean that the dissolution of the unity of the self is beyond the pale of experience. I draw on reported cases of schizophrenia in Ronald Laing's *The Divided Self* and on Heidegger's description of anxiety in *What is Metaphysics?* to show that such a dissolution is a possible experience and that, consequently, possible experience does not depend on the unity of the self as a necessary condition of possibility. The target of my argument is Dan Zahavi's transcendental phenomenological theory of experience in *Self-Awareness and Alterity* according to which there is no experience without the unity of the first person.

In section 2, I shed light on the distinction Heidegger draws between *perishing* and *demise* in *Being and Time*. Turning to Heidegger's claim that *death is in each case mine*, I argue in section 3 that a first-person ownership of the relation to death is impossible.

In section 4, I consider another way of reading Heidegger's claim. It can be read as saying that death singularizes the *who*. I draw on Paul Ricoeur's distinction between *ipse-* and *idem-*identity in *Oneself as Another* to clarify what I mean by the distinction between singularization and individuation.

In section 5, I argue that the relation to death can bring about the collapse of the 'mineness' of existence and that this collapse is a possible experience, contrary to what Zahavi suggests in *Self-Awareness and Alterity*.

In section 6, I turn to Derrida's *Aporias*. That text is akin to the spirit of Zahavi's transcendentalism in some respects, insofar as it is intent on revealing non-revisable constraints on possible experience. Much like Zahavi, Derrida contends that the relation to death cannot appear as such. But in another respect, Derrida makes allowances for it in friendship and mourning, as does Heidegger with the notion of anticipation in *Being and Time*.

Accordingly, in this chapter, I argue that Heidegger and Derrida's reflections on death can be seen as calling for a rethinking of the sense of *consciousness* or *experience* in transcendental phenomenology beyond the unity of the first person.

2. Perishing and demise

In section 49 of *Being and Time*, Heidegger argues that the existential interpretation of being-toward-death is ontologically prior to the biological understanding of death as an event that is bound up with the processes of life and to the anthropological and ethnological study of mortuary rites, burial or cremation practices, the domestic or public cult of the dead, practices of mourning and so on.

Biological explanations of the causes of death in plants, animals or humans, of their longevity, growth or reproductive cycles, presuppose an ontology of life. The science of life would not know what to apply itself to; the extension of its field would be left undetermined if it did not operate with a preliminary understanding of the essence of life. Its understanding of life, whether as a physico-chemical mechanism or as a movement of self-organization, guides, in turn, its understanding of death and anticipates its approach to it. But whatever the basic concepts the science of life and its ontology appropriate, they understand death – for evident reasons – as the end of life. Death is defined on the basis of life and the formal-ontological consideration of the kind of end that constitutes death, the meaning or essence of death, is left by the wayside.

No doubt, death signifies the end. But that can mean any number of things. Depending on whether the word is taken as a noun or verb, *end* can mean cessation, stopping or fulfilment; it can mean to limit, the limit or to be limited; to vanish or come to a close; the goal or reaching the goal, and so on. As long as the meaning of *end* is left undetermined, no decisive and unequivocal headway seems promising in the ontology of life.

That is why Heidegger can say that the concepts of life and death in biology and the ontology of life 'need to be sketched by the ontology of Dasein' (*BT* 291), which explores death in its formal-ontological constitution by reference to Dasein's kind of being. Heidegger is well aware of 'the peculiar *formality* and emptiness of any ontological characterization'. But this 'must not blind us to the rich and complicated structure of the phenomenon' (*BT* 292).

Similarly, anthropological studies of burial and cremation practices, of mortuary rites and funerary customs, presuppose a conception of death. Besides, such studies inform us more about a community's self-understanding than about the essence of death. As Heidegger notes, most likely with reference to Ernst Cassirer's *The Philosophy of Symbolic Forms*, 'the ways in which death is taken among primitive peoples, and their ways of comporting themselves to it in magic and cult, illuminate primarily the understanding of *Dasein*; but the interpretation of this understanding already requires an existential analytic and a corresponding conception of death' (*BT* 291–2).

This brief and somewhat commonplace analysis of the order of priority or *founding* between the use of the concept of death in biology, the ontology of life and fundamental ontology – commonplace, at any rate, within transcendental phenomenology that Heidegger, I believe, does not entirely abandon in this period – leads to some of the most controversial and remarkable statements in *Being and Time*, statements that we have not yet finished interpreting.[2]

The existential understanding of death as being-toward-death is reducible neither to a universal structure of life nor to a particular cultural signification. Dasein's dying (*sterben*) embodies an ontological structure that exceeds the horizons of life and spirit. On the one hand, dying cannot be identified with a biological process. If Dasein dies, or rather, because it can die, it 'never perishes'. On the other hand, its death doubtless has a cultural and medico-legal sense in the world. That is to say that Dasein demises (*ablebt*). But it can do so only because and on condition that it can die. Dasein can 'demise only as long as it is dying' (*BT* 291).

Reading these passages in bewilderment, David Farrell Krell (1992: 92–3) wonders in *Daimon Life* whether the distinction between *dying*, *demise* and *perishing* is 'wholly specious'. He adds that the introduction of the notion of *demise* 'marks the demise of existential-ontological demarcation as such. That introduction constitutes one of the many ends of fundamental ontology.' That is presumably because Heidegger, in Krell's eyes, is unable to sustain the distinction between *demise* and *perishing* for very long. As Krell (1992: 98) notes a few pages later, '*Ableben* slips unobtrusively into the position formerly occupied by biological-medical *Verenden*. *Ableben* will now have to do, not with inappropriateness, but with biology and medicine!'

Dasein verendet nie. Dasein never perishes. *Verenden* is a term that Heidegger reserves for that which is living, *das Lebendem* (*BT* 291), usually, more narrowly, for animal life. Plant life rarely gets a mention in Heidegger's works. The difference between *verenden* and *sterben* is clearly not reducible to a terminological point. Something substantive must be meant by it.

Let us suppose that Dasein is alive. That cannot be more than a supposition. Heidegger's categorical denial that Dasein perishes opens the possibility that not every entity that is of the measure of Dasein is a living thing. A Dasein endowed with a non-biological constitution – a transcendental machine – is not inconceivable.[3] However, if Dasein is alive, must it not perish?

Perhaps what Heidegger has in mind is that life and, in consequence, the end of living beings, perishing, do not enter Dasein's ontological constitution. That seems to be true on the face of it as well. Being-toward-death does not vary even though Dasein's physico-chemical makeup varies over time. Death always impends for me, whether I am young or old, healthy or ill, male or female.

Correlatively – although that is how Heidegger is usually read – perishing doesn't enter its ontological constitution, *Dasein verendet nie*, since whatever perishes has no access to death and what defines *Dasein* is precisely such access. This is how Heidegger describes the meaning of *perishing* in a lecture in 1950, *Das Ding*.

> Only man dies. The animal perishes. It has death neither ahead of itself (*vor sich*) nor behind it (*hinter sich*). ... We ... call mortals mortals – not because their earthly life comes to an end, but because they are capable of death as death. (*PLT* 178)

To be alive is not a sufficient condition to be of the measure of Dasein. Dasein will perish if it has an organic form. It will perish not on account of its Daseinhood but on account of the fact that it is alive. An entity must have access to death as such to satisfy the condition of Daseinhood. What Heidegger probably means, then, when he says that *Dasein verendet nie*, is that Dasein never perishes *qua* Dasein.

Ableben aber kann des Dasein nur solange, als er sterbt. But Dasein can demise only as long as it is dying. What does Heidegger mean by this? Is it truly perplexing, as Krell (1992: 98) seems to think? Does it cause the distinction between *Ableben* and *Verenden* and, correlatively, between Dasein and the animal, to collapse, along with the possibility of the existential analytic?

I think that Taylor Carman (2005: 290) is on the right track when he says in *Authenticity* that the distinction between *dying* and *demising* is best seen as marking a difference between understanding one's death from the first and from the third person. Since the 'animal' does not relate to its end in any way whatsoever, we can say that it *perishes*.[4]

I can understand death as a possibility that is mine in every case. Or I can understand it as an issue that is common to many.

> In Dasein's public way of interpreting, it is said that 'one dies' (*man stirbt*), because everyone else and oneself can talk himself into saying that 'in no case is it I myself', for this 'one' is the 'nobody'. Dying is levelled off to an occurrence which reaches Dasein, to be sure, but belongs to nobody in particular.... Dying, which is essentially mine in such a way that no one can be my representative (*unvertretbar*), is perverted into an event of public occurrence which the 'they' encounters. (*BT* 297)

Death is always in play as a non-substitutable end for Dasein. No one can remove, replace or displace it by means of a symbolic or real sacrifice. It is an end in which no other has a share. It is, like an absolute secret, absolutely unshareable.[5] As Heidegger says without circumlocution in his 1925 lecture *History of the Concept of Time*, 'There is no such thing as death in general' (*HCT* 313).

Doubtless, there is such a thing as 'death in general'. But that thing is there for *das Man*. I objectify my death as a concern that is common to many, or as an occurrence in the world that has a legal, medical or cultural meaning. I regard my death as an event that is in no way different from the death of the other, any other.

If *dying* is always one's ownmost, proper, or *eigene* end, if it is an end to which Dasein has a pre-objective access, that is, unmediated by cultural institutions and significations, an end to which it can attest as its ownmost, proper possibility, *demising* concerns everyman. It refers Dasein to the other's death or to its own from the standpoint of the institutions and practices of its culture.

Ableben aber kann des Dasein nur solange, als er sterbt. Far from being confusing as Krell seems to believe, this statement must mean that I would not be able to relate to death in the third person (*one dies*) unless I was able to relate to it in the first person.

The distinction between *dying* and *demising* seems clear enough on the surface. But it raises a question. Do *dying* and *demising* mean the same thing under two different descriptions? Or do they intend two different things?

Heidegger's talk of demise in the text is not always very precise. He associates it with the cessation of Dasein's 'physiological' life, with the legal-medical certification of death, with the '"typology" of "dying"' that is concerned with the taxonomy of psychological experiences (*Erlebnisse*) of dying persons (*BT* 291), and with an occurrence in the public world of *das Man* (*BT* 301). By contrast, *dying* is described as 'the possibility of the absolute impossibility of Dasein' (*BT* 294).

This suggests that *dying* and *demising* do not mean or intend the same phenomenon under two different descriptions. They mean different things in more or less the same way as originary time, that is, the temporalization of ecstatic temporality, refers to something other than metric time, understood as a succession of nows, even though the latter derives its meaning as *time* from the former.

In other words, once it is understood as an event in the world that is common to all of mankind – classically instanced in the major premise of a categorical syllogism, 'All humans are mortal' – *dying* is no longer what it is, Dasein's *eigenste* and *unvertretbare* end. But that just makes it more urgent to ask what *dying* means.

3. Is dying possible?

Is a first-person ownership of the relation to death possible?

Expressions such as *authentic* (*eigentlich*) *dying* or *authentic being-toward-death* are no doubt pleonasms. *Dying* is an end to which the adjectives *one's own* (*eigen*) and *ownmost* (*eigenste*) intrinsically belong. Heidegger writes:

> By its essence, death is in each case mine, in so far as it 'is' at all. (*BT* 284)

When death is spoken of inauthentically, it is thought of as a common occurrence in the world. But when it is spoken of properly, it is thought of as something that is neither common nor worldly. Jean-François Courtine (1991: 80) observes in *Voice of Conscience and Call of Being* that the 'only authentic utterance in which *Dasein* finds expression' is 'I shall die, I must die.' We can say, with greater precision, that an authentic utterance that gives expression to Dasein will always use singular pronouns, *my* death, *your* death. Dasein owns its relation to death in a privileged, first-person way.

To be sure, that is true not only of the relation to death. It is true also of existence and of experience. Existence and experience are hardly conceivable save as owned in the first person. *I am having a perception of this red cube. I exist.* The author of my existence and of my experience may be unknown to me. It may be unidentifiable. But they cannot fail to have an owner.

That is not to deny that first-person ownership is, for the most part, neutralized, suppressed, or forgotten by *das Man*, such that existence and experience, including death, appear as impersonal causal events in nature or as culturally mediated significations.

In the sentence cited above, Heidegger qualifies the statement that 'death is in every case mine' with the clause 'in so far as it "is" at all'. Why does he qualify it in that way? Is he having doubts about ascribing mineness to death?

Der Tot ist, sofern er 'ist', wesenmäßig je der meine. Heidegger is hesitant about using the verb *being* in the case of death. The word no doubt applies to experience and existence. They are different kinds of entities. They are determinable as such or such. But is death an entity? Is it determinable in a certain way or against a particular horizon? Does it not arrive from beyond the horizons of meaning that Dasein projects or the contexts of understanding in which it approaches entities and others?

If the word *death* does not denote an entity, if it is not the concept of a determinable object, if *death* gives me nothing to think about, then I am not sure that there is a first-person ownership of the relation to death. Can the *I* relate in the first person to what is not an entity without losing its unity and hold on itself? I am not sure.

Besides, far from endowing the first-person with a unity that would enable it to unify itself in the diversity of experience, the relation to death dissolves every kind of unity and identity. *Death*, supposing it has a meaning, signifies the dissolution of the unity of the self, the disintegration of the identity of the concept, the collapse of the unity of the name. It is the non-contingent limit of language and thought.

That is why there is no concept of death. That is why the name is an empty signifier. But that is also why a first-person ownership of the relation to death is a *de jure* impossibility.[6]

Does it mean that there is only a third-person ownership of the relation to death, an objectified death, or a relation to the death of the other in mourning?[7] That is the conclusion that Derrida will come to in *Aporias* in his reading of Heidegger, as I show in section 6.

Maurice Blanchot remarks in the *Space of Literature* that death does not happen to the *I*. It happens to someone. Like writing, dying is a passivity without reserve that deprives the *I* of its activity, reducing it to the impersonal *one*.

> [H]e who dies is anonymous, and anonymity is the guise in which the ungraspable, the unlimited, the unsituated is most dangerously affirmed among us. (Blanchot, 1982: 241)[8]

That is a lesson Heidegger too will learn two years after the publication of *Being and Time* in his 1929 inaugural lecture *What is Metaphysics?* It means that the dissolution of the unity of the *I* before death is a possible experience and that, in consequence, the unity of the *I* is not a necessary constraint on possible experience. That is what I show in section 5 against Zahavi's transcendentalism in *Self-Awareness and Alterity*.

Heidegger says in *Being and Time* that death 'knows no measure (*Maß*) at all, no more or less (*mehr oder minder*), but signifies the possibility of the measureless impossibility of existence' (*BT* 307). The category of measure, of the more and the less, does not apply here. Or if it does apply to the relation to death, then we must think of it as Dasein's opening to the exorbitant, the impossible or the sublime.

Death is the possibility that gives Dasein access to the impossibility of existence. The impossibility of existence is Dasein's non-presence, its departure from the world, its final farewell (*Abschied*) (*Zo* 184). Why is that ultimate farewell exorbitant or without measure? Death is the limit of its existence. But there is no limit to its non-existence. Its departure from the world is absolute and singular at the same time.

How can Dasein own the relation to that absence in the first-person? No doubt, that absence is not there as long as Dasein is there. As the Epicureans say, if I am, then death is not; if death is, then I am not. When Dasein is there, its death is there only as a future. But that is a future that is discontinuous with the present.[9] My eventual absence is not thinkable as a modality of the present, as a past- or future-present. It is not an event that I will be able to recall once I will have died. Nor is it an event that will become present to me or that I can expect in advance. I cannot be ready for something that has never been and that will never be present to me.

But if my departure from the world is a future that is unthinkable as a modality of the present, then it is by the same token unthinkable as a modification of being as presence (see Chapter 3.2 for the connection between being and time, presence and the present: the comprehension of the former is based on the latter). It exceeds the categories of being as modifications of presence. Now *possibility* is a category of being. It is a modification of presence. Hence the question arises whether death is possible. 'Is my death possible?' Derrida (1993: 21) wonders in *Aporias*.

4. Singularization

Der Tot ist, sofern er 'ist', wesenmäßig je der meine. Death is in each case mine, if it 'is' at all. This sentence can mean something other than that Dasein has a first-person ownership of the relation to death. The *Jemeinigkeit* of death can also mean that dying singularizes Dasein.

I am not sure that it is accurate to say that it *individuates* Dasein. An *individual*, in the strict sense, denotes an indivisible something like an atom, and Dasein is not an individual in that strict sense, whether as soul, substance, ego or person. These are all instances of things that are indivisible. Paul Ricoeur's distinction between the identity of the self (*ipse*) and the identity of the same (*idem*) in *Oneself as Another* goes some way towards clarifying what I have in mind with the distinction between singularity and individuality.[10]

Following Kant, Ricoeur claims that permanence in time is the transcendental criterion for numerical identity. If I want to determine whether the object of my perception is a substance, that is, a *what* or, in Kantian terms, something that is distinct from the perceiving self, then I must consider whether it is permanent in time.

Now Ricoeur argues that character conforms to that criterion. Character constitutes a person's numerical identity. One's second nature consists of acquired and sedimented habits and dispositions that remain relatively unchanged through life. Character must then be distinguished from another 'form of permanence in time' that is not merely the schema of substance and that relates to 'the question "who?" inasmuch as it is irreducible to any question of "what?"' (Ricoeur, 1992: 118). As an example of the former question, Ricoeur mentions keeping one's word.

> [That] expresses a *self-constancy* which cannot be inscribed, as character was, within the dimension of something in general but solely within the dimension of the 'who?'. (Ricoeur, 1992: 123)

When I promise my partner to do something I make myself accountable to her. She also counts on me. She expects that I will remain true to my word even if, in the face of adversity, I was forced to act out of character repeatedly and my character was to gradually change. The constancy of the self is, in consequence, distinct from the permanence of character. According to Ricoeur, it is grounded in an ethics of responsibility.

> [*Ipse*-identity] is represented by the essentially ethical notion of self-constancy. Self-constancy is for each person that manner of conducting himself or herself so that others can *count on* that person. Because someone is counting on me, I am *accountable for* my actions before another. The term 'responsibility' unites both meanings: 'counting on' and 'being accountable for'. (Ricoeur, 1992: 165)

Is the dimension of the *who* accurately staked out that way? I am not sure.

It must be asked, in the first place, what the *who* precisely picks out. The answer, standardly, is that it picks out a person rather than a thing. But who is the proper subject of the *who*? Is it someone who makes herself responsible before the other in the institution of the promise? Or is it someone who makes herself responsible for her existence, granted that she has become mindful of the fact that she can die at any moment and that her existence is, accordingly, non-replaceable?

Let me put the question otherwise. What singularizes existence first of all? What makes it *mine* in the first place? Is it my ethical responsibility before the other?

There are good reasons to think so. For if that responsibility is non-transferable, if no other can take my place in fulfilling my ethical duty to the other, then that duty or responsibility highlights the non-replaceability or uniqueness of my existence.

Now the thing about uniqueness is that it is irreducible to a concept. In particular, it is irreducible to the concept of identity, whether to the concept of specific or that of numerical identity.[11] *Uniqueness* means absolute difference, Levinas says to Raoul Mortley (1991: 16) in an interview. It is like an intuition without concept.

Or shall we say that what singularizes existence, first of all, is one's exposure to death rather than the responsibility for the other?

I am not sure how to decide that question. In whatever way it is decided, whether in favour of Ricoeur (or Levinas) or Heidegger, it is clear that the terms in which Ricoeur poses the issue precludes him from accurately demarcating the *who* from the *what*. The issue is posed in terms of 'two models of permanence in time'. The suspicion, therefore, is that the *what* and the *who* are determined as two species of *permanence in time*. As the schema of substance, it follows that selfhood and sameness are conceived as two instances of substance. Contrary to what Ricoeur desires to think in terms of his distinction between *ipse-* and *idem*-identity, self-constancy and character constitute two instances of the *what*.

No such suspicion arises with Heidegger. For it is not by reference to two modes of presence that the *who* and the *what* are distinguished in *Being and Time*. It is by reference to the imminence of death, the future, that the *who* appears as a distinct dimension of Dasein. If the *who* is the site of singularization, of the non-replaceability of existence, the *what* is the site of individuation, of the constitution of the numerical identity of substance. Only what is absolute (non-relational) and singular – death in its imminence – can singularize absolutely.

The various characteristics that Heidegger uses to describe *dying* in section 50 of *Being and Time* are in effect characteristics of imminence, *bevorstehen*.

> [Death] reveals itself as that *possibility which is one's ownmost, which is non-relational, and which is not to be outstripped.* As such, death is something *distinctively* impending (*Bevorstand*). (*BT* 294)

Dying is an end before which Dasein always already stands. It is not a *telos*, a potentiality whose actualization fulfils and perfects Dasein.

> With ripeness, the fruit *fulfills* itself. But is the death at which Dasein arrives, a fulfillment in this sense? (*BT* 288)

Let us suppose that Dasein attains a state of maturity in the world in the Aristotelian sense. It is perfect and whole. It is engaged in fulfilling its elected potentialities-for-being-a-self. Nevertheless, its end does not cease approaching. Its end is not a potentiality that calls for being actualized or exercised like a habit or virtue. Its end is, properly speaking, *atelic*. It can have no reality or actuality for Dasein, no mode of presence, save as what is to come at any moment. Death is imminence pure and simple.

As long as Dasein exists, it cannot finish dying. It is as if dying was interminable for Dasein, as if death was always not yet or no longer there, and the gap, in truth infinitesimal, between existence and nonexistence never ceased shrinking without closing.

That is why ending for Dasein cannot signify being *at* an end (*Zu-Ende-sein*) but, rather, being *towards* the end (*Sein zum Ende*). Death's imminent approach discloses the dimension of the *to come* (*Zu-kunft*). It reveals the future on which Dasein projects itself in anticipation. The self-projection on death in anticipatory resoluteness manifests Dasein's being-ahead-of-itself. This *"ahead-of-itself" is what first of all makes such a Being-towards-the-end possible'* (*BT* 303).

Ricoeur (1992: 123) is right to say that the self-constancy of Dasein finds its meaning in anticipatory resoluteness.

> Existentially, '*Self-constancy*' signifies nothing other than anticipatory resoluteness. (*BT* 369)

Self-constancy in Heidegger means neither self-sufficiency (autarky or independence) nor the ethical responsibility to the other accomplished in the promise. It signifies Dasein's ability to come back to itself as the same, its power of self-constitution. Heidegger writes in the *Zollikon Seminars*:

> The constancy of the self is proper to itself in the sense that the self is always able to come back to itself and always finds itself still the same in its sojourn. (*Zo* 175)

As I show in greater detail in the next section, this power of self-constitution does not rest on a solid foundation. In resoluteness, Dasein projects itself on death before returning to itself as the same. As a consequence, it is in principle vulnerable to suffer loss of self, anxiety and absolute disorientation. Its social and practical identity is never without some trace or evidence that it is, in its very being, related to death. After all, the reason why its existence is always an issue for it is that it is affectively aware that it can die at any moment.

5. Schizophrenia

I have argued that a first-person ownership of the relation to death is not possible (see section 3). If that argument is sound, then the question arises whether a first-person ownership of one's existence is possible in the face of death. Or does anxiety before death bring to naught the mineness of existence?

Heidegger seems to be in two minds about this. In *Being and Time*, he sees the possibility of death as authenticating his description of existence as a thrown projection that is uniquely mine in each case. In *What is Metaphysics?*, the possibility of death or anxiety appears as the complete undoing of mineness.

In the second chapter of Division II of *Being and Time* (see Chapter 2.4 for a detailed analysis), Heidegger argues that Dasein can own its existence in the first person (authentically) only if it can own its being-toward-death in the first person (as its ownmost possibility of being).

Conscience calls Dasein from its fallenness in the mundane world of *das Man*. It calls it to assume responsibility for itself. Dasein is answerable to itself because it has been entrusted to itself: it finds itself disclosed as an entity in the world, that is, projected as a possibility of being (say) a carpenter or teacher, a parent, a sister, etc. Conscience calls it to take responsibility for this disclosure or projection since its non-replaceable existence is at stake in it.

That is something that becomes conspicuous to Dasein in anxiety. In anxiety, Dasein is present to itself as an entity that is both disclosed in the world and disclosive of the world. It has itself as an entity that is both projected and projecting.[12]

> *Here the disclosure and the disclosed are existentially selfsame in such a way that in the latter the world has been disclosed as world, and Being-in has been disclosed as a potentiality-for-Being which is singularized, pure, and thrown.* (BT 233)

Disclosed as thrown projection, Dasein now faces the choice of having to choose itself. What it chooses in choosing *itself* is not a factical possibility like being a carpenter or teacher. Anyone can be a carpenter or teacher. What is uniquely its own is the formal structure of existence, namely thrown projection. That is what it must choose and own as if for the first time rather than continue to take for granted its *transcendental constitution*.

Dasein can do so, Heidegger insists, to the extent that it projects a factical possibility on death. Why death? Because death removes the content of that factical possibility, it renders it insignificant and brings in relief its formal structure. It shows that I remain naïve so long as I continue to think that to be a teacher is a social role in the world or a natural station in society rather than a *projection* into which I have been *thrown*, and for which I am responsible, since projection is an *accomplishment of mine*.

It is thus by focusing my factical possibilities on death that I can start owning the factical situation that I find myself in explicitly as mine. 'Courage for anxiety in the face of death' (BT 298) makes possible an authentic appropriation of existence.

In *What is Metaphysics?*, Heidegger is more cautious. He suggests that there is an alternative to the three possibilities, sketched out in *Being and Time*, of responding to anxiety:

(a) I flee from anxiety before death by immersing myself in the world. I live my existence as *one* lives it, that is, by understanding myself from what I do or from how others perceive me. That is self-evasion in the face of anxiety and death or inauthenticity.

(b) I am brave for anxiety. I am thus able to appropriate existence explicitly as mine in given factical situations.

(c) I am indifferent to anxiety before death. It does not affect me or, more precisely, anxiety remains latent. Here I understand my existence in a modally undifferentiated way, that is, this self-understanding is not explicitly articulated from either the first- or the third-person, authentically or inauthentically.

Heidegger writes in *Being and Time*:

> This *potentiality-for-being*, as one that is in each case *mine*, is free for authenticity and inauthenticity or for a mode in which neither of these has been differentiated. (*BT* 275)

In *What is Metaphysics?*, Heidegger suggests that in addition to these three possibilities, which depend on the fact that existence is mine in each case, anxiety can be so overwhelming and unsettling that it can bring about the collapse of mineness. What appears in such a situation is a singular existence that is unclaimed by the self and that remains, in consequence, anonymous.

The aim of *What is Metaphysics?* is also different from Chapter 2 of Division II of *Being and Time* where death and anxiety appear in the course of an argument that is designed to show that an ontic-existentiell attestation of an ontological structure is possible. Heidegger delivered his inaugural lecture before the faculties of the natural and social sciences at the University of Freiburg in 1929. He argues that it is not possible to talk about entities without having some understanding of the kind of entities they are and also of how they are. That understanding does not have to be articulated in concepts or propositions in order to talk about entities. It is a general presupposition, a necessary condition of possibility, of any meaningful talk about entities. I must have some vague or inexplicit grasp of the *is*, for instance, if I am able to distinguish between the *is* of predication and the *is* of identity in the sentences *Socrates is wise*, and *Socrates is a human being*.

Another way of saying the same thing is that there is no science without metaphysics. Science represents a particular way of talking about entities, whereas metaphysics is concerned with the being of entities. Heidegger then argues that the understanding of the being of entities, whether or not it is richly articulated or explicit to itself, presupposes, in turn, an understanding of the difference between being and entities. What is that difference? That difference is what comes to light in anxiety. It is Dasein.

Anxiety leaves us hanging because it induces the slipping away of beings as a whole. This implies that we ourselves – we humans who are in being – in the midst of beings slip away from ourselves. At bottom therefore it is not as though 'you' or 'I' feel ill at ease; rather, it is this way for some 'one'. In the altogether unsettling experience of this hovering where there is nothing to hold onto, pure Da-sein is all that is still there. (*BW* 101)

Daher ist im Grunde nicht 'dir' und 'mir' unheimlich, sondern 'einem' ist es so. The sudden collapse of meaning in anxiety is radically disabling, Heidegger tells us. It is so unsettling that the *I* vanishes. Put differently, the collapse of meaning is an experience that can no longer be owned in the first or third persons. All that remains when the world grows dark in anxiety, when language and meaning withdraw, and the ability to refer to the self or to the other has been quashed, is the experience of being there pure and simple.

But is an experience like that possible? Does not the possibility of experience depend on the possibility of owning it in the first person, as Kant and Husserl show in different ways?

That is what Dan Zahavi argues in *Self-Awareness and Alterity*. He says that there is no type of experience that lacks a first personal mode of givenness. By *first personal givenness*, Zahavi does not mean self-identification through criteria such as name, sex, physical appearance, family, nationality, profession, knowledge or memories. None of these third personal characteristics are necessary in order to think of or to refer to oneself as *I*.

Suppose someone is suffering from amnesia. She is immobilized in a dark room and is ignorant of her biography. She is still capable of being self-aware and saying *I do not remember anything*.

[The *I*] refers without attributing any specific property to the entity in question, and my awareness of myself is consequently not mediated by the awareness of any identifying property. (Zahavi, 1999: 7)

[The *I*] cannot fail to refer to the object it purports to refer to, and one can consequently speak of its *ontological and referential priority* over all names and descriptions. (Zahavi, 1999: 3–4)

The self that I am aware of when I utter the sentence *I do not remember anything* does not exist apart from the pre-reflexive experience of being unable to remember anything. It is neither the transcendental ego that unifies the goings on of the empirical ego nor is it the empirical ego, an object posited in the world.

The subject or self referred to in *self*-awareness is not something apart from or beyond the experience, nor is it a new and further experience, but simply a feature or function of its givenness. If the experience is given to me originarily, in a first-personal mode of presentation, it is experienced as my experience, otherwise not. (Zahavi, 1999: 12)

Zahavi contends that there is an irremovable centre or orientation to experience. There is a first-person to which experiences are always given. At bottom, an experience is given to *me*, or it is not an experience.

Is Zahavi correct? Is an experience such as Heidegger describes in *What is Metaphysics?* inconceivable?

Let me consider cases of depersonalization. Someone who suffers from that condition believes that others control their thoughts or that there is someone else who is thinking their thoughts. Doesn't that suggest that there is a mode of experience that lacks givenness in the first-person?

Zahavi is sceptical of the way such experiences are described.

[Although] the experiences of a subject suffering from depersonalization have been described as experiences which lack the peculiar quality of *my-ness*, one might question the accuracy of this description.

Depersonalized experiences appear strange and intrusive. But, Zahavi continues, 'They cannot lack this formal kind of my-ness, since the subject is aware that it is he himself rather than somebody else who experiences these foreign thoughts' (Zahavi, 1997: 154).

That argument is hardly convincing. It merely asserts what needs to be proved. That is that the subject *is* aware of being the owner of these foreign thoughts. Zahavi's assertion contradicts a patient's self-description that Ronald Laing reports in *The Divided Self*.

I forgot myself at the Ice Carnival the other night. I was so absorbed in looking at it that I forgot what time it was and who and where I was. When I suddenly realized I hadn't been thinking about myself I was frightened to death. The unreality feeling came. I must never forget myself for a single minute. I watch the clock and keep busy, or else I won't know who I am. (Laing, 1969: 109)

The patient is recalling that she was not aware of who she was and of where she was at the Ice Carnival. It is as if, whilst being there, she was not there, as if she had become a living corpse, experiencing a 'death', an eclipse of 'myself', which had brought on the feeling of 'unreality'. That is why she now insists: 'I must never forget *myself* for a single minute' (my emphasis).

Zahavi does not give us any good reason for thinking that this patient has misdescribed her experience.

It might be argued that some experiences of depersonalization are experiences of extreme self-objectification. Zahavi observes:

> The subject is so obsessively preoccupied with his experiences that they are gradually transformed and substantialized into objectlike entities, which are then experienced as alien, intrusive, involuntary, and independent.

Self-objectification is a form of *reflective* self-awareness. That presupposes the first personal givenness of pre-reflexive self-awareness (Zahavi, 1999: 156).

It certainly seems as if a depersonalized experience is objectified in an act of reflection. But that does not capture the full extent of the experience. I find it odd, in the first place, that Zahavi does not once mention Heidegger's account of anxiety. All of the experiences of depersonalization that Laing reports in *The Divided Self* (on which Zahavi draws) are experiences of anxiety.

In the second place, the schizoid doubtless has a heightened awareness of her outward behaviour. She regards it as meaningless, insubstantial, unreal or mechanical. But that is a defence mechanism against anxiety before death. Death is understood by some patients as loss of self, as becoming one with the world (Laing, 1969: 99; see the case of James), as the kind of sacral fusion that Hölderlin describes at the start of *Hyperion* and whose loss he mourns in the remainder of the poem:

> To be one with all that lives, to return in blessed self-oblivion into the All of nature. (Hölderlin, 2011: 13)

Let me first consider what fails to function in depersonalization. Depersonalization might be described, in a first approximation, in Rimbaud's phrase as 'I is an other.' Existence is not or is no longer mine. What does that mean?

It does not mean that my existence has now become an object to me or that it is now under the control of some alien voice. The schizoid lives under a constant threat. That is that her existence is slipping away from her. Mineness is always on the verge of collapsing. It is as if her ability to project her existence *as* hers was about to fail.

That is what Laing suggests when he describes the depersonalized subject as 'ontologically insecure'. That is a subject whose identity is so weak and feeble that she is pulled in contrary directions.

On the one hand, she lacks the conviction that she is real. Contrary to what Descartes believes, she cannot be sure that she exists when she thinks. She needs to be in the presence of others who can be aware of her, since that alone can give her the reassurance she needs: to know that she does indeed exist and is real. She believes that *I am, I exist*, is a true proposition that applies to her, not each time that it is put forward by her mind, but so long as others are conscious of her. She thus makes herself visible to others so as to protect herself from the overwhelming feeling of being unreal, insubstantial, a nullity.

At the same time, however, to be visible to others is to be exposed to danger. The danger is that others are aware of her just as she is aware of herself, that is, as an insubstantial thing, a nullity.

Accordingly, the subject de-subjectifies herself. She makes herself invisible to herself and to others as well in an act of self-oblivion. She blends with the landscape like a chameleon and becomes one with what there is.

> Indeed, considered biologically, the very fact of being visible exposes an animal to the risk of attack from its enemies, and no animal is without enemies. Being visible is therefore a basic biological risk; being invisible is a basic biological defence. We all employ some form of camouflage. (Laing, 1969: 110)

The schizoid lives in a conflicted and tensed state. She needs to be visible and invisible at the same time. She needs to be visible to others so that she can be convinced that she exists. She needs to be invisible to others and to herself so that she can be convinced that others don't see her as she sees herself.

That is how a patient described her experience:

> *It struck me that if I stared long enough at the environment that I would blend with it and disappear just as if the place was empty and I had disappeared. It is as if you get yourself to feel you don't know who you are or where you are.... I would just* be walking along and felt that I had blended with the landscape. Then I would get frightened and repeat my name over and over again to bring me back to life, so to speak. (Laing, 1969: 110)

By blending with the landscape, Laing comments, the patient lost 'her autonomous identity, in fact, she lost her self'. She did not faint. Consciousness does not disappear when the self disappears. Instead, the disappearance of the self seems to bring about an intensified awareness, an acute anxiety that is blinding and that leaves one speechless. It is as if the marked differentiation between entities, their distinct outline and boundaries, suddenly dissolved and what remained was the presence of an undifferentiated whole, a void or '*empty place*', as the patient puts it, in which the distinction between *I* and *you*, and *self* and *world* has totally vanished.

To a certain extent, this camouflage and blending with the environment is a game, a ruse or pretence. But that is also where the trouble lies, according to Laing:

> The individual may find that the pretense has been in the pretending and that, in a more real way than he had bargained for, he has actually lapsed into that very state of non-being he has so much dreaded, in which he has become stripped of his sense of autonomy, reality, life, identity, and from which he may not find it possible to regain his foothold 'in' life again by the simple repetition of his name. (Laing, 1969: 111)

We stand, then, before two options. Let us say that we agree with Zahavi that an *experience* is necessarily given first-personally. It follows that none of what Laing reports and none of what Heidegger says about anxiety qualifies as a description of experience.

I have grave doubts about that. Not least because Zahavi's fairly conservative transcendental phenomenological notion of experience seems to force him to reject reported descriptions of experience for no apparent reason other than that they do not fit the theory.

The other option is that we acknowledge that *givenness in the first-person* or *self-reference* is not an irreducible and necessary feature of experience. Anxiety, the relation to death, and schizophrenia articulate the absolute limit of transcendental philosophy. They show that the possibility of consciousness is not necessarily constrained by the unity of the first-person.[13]

On the basis of the evidence adduced in this section, it is reasonable to assume that mineness can collapse in anxiety before death. Isn't that what it means to be mortal? Exposed to death as death, the sense of things can fail, leaving me unable to think and say *I, you*. In such a situation, all that remains is the sheer fact of being there.

6. Mourning

Heidegger claims that I can own existence in the first-person only if I can own the relation to death in the first-person. Dasein can be authentically itself (*eigentlich es selbst*) only if it can become free for its own mortality (*eigenen Tod*) (*BT* 308). Since it is impossible to own the relation to death in the first-person, as I have shown in section 3, I cannot see how it is possible to own existence in the first-person before death.

Instead of enabling it to unify itself in an act of self-appropriation, anxiety before death tends to fracture the unity of the self, as I showed in section 5 and as Heidegger acknowledges in *What is Metaphysics?*. That must mean that the courage in the face of anxiety that makes possible an authentic appropriation of existence is a theoretical construct in *Being and Time* and not merely a somewhat rare and exotic possibility.

At the same time, I argued against Zahavi that the fracturing of the unity of the self is a possible experience, providing that the sense of *experience* is broadened and is not unduly restricted to *first-personal givenness*.

Now Zahavi is not the first to have ruled out the possibility of such an experience. In *Aporias*, Derrida argues that access to death as death is not possible. As a result, it is not possible to distinguish Dasein from the 'animal' and the existential analytic falls to the ground. If access to death is impossible, then Dasein will perish like the 'animal'. Let me cite Derrida's passage from *Aporias* in full.

> The impossibility of existing or of *Dasein* that Heidegger speaks of under the name of 'death' is the disappearance, the end, the annihilation of the '*as such*', of the possibility of the relation to the phenomenon *as such* or to the phenomenon of the '*as such*'.... According to Heidegger, it is therefore, the impossibility of the 'as such' that, *as such*, would be possible to Dasein and not to any form of entity and living thing. But if the impossibility of the 'as such' is indeed the impossibility of the 'as such', it is also what cannot appear as such. Indeed, this relation to the disappearing as such of the 'as such' ... is also the characteristic common *both* to the inauthentic *and* to the authentic forms of the existence of *Dasein*, common to all experiences of death (properly dying, perishing, and demising), and also, outside of *Dasein*, common to all living things in general. Common characteristic does not mean homogeneity, but rather the impossibility of an absolutely pure and rigorously uncrossable limit ... between an existential analysis of death and a fundamental anthropo-theology, and moreover between anthropological cultures of death and animal cultures of death. (Derrida, 1993: 75)

Derrida seems to be saying that Heidegger's thinking of death in *Being and Time* is caught in a double bind. Either death can appear as such or it cannot. If it can appear as such, then it was never what it was supposed to be, notably, the inapparent, or what is to come at any moment, since a death that can appear as such carries the sense of *demising* or *perishing*. It is the other's death or the 'animal's', an objectified death.

But if death cannot appear as such, then Dasein finds itself in the same predicament as the 'animal', since death can also not appear to it. The key sentence in the passage seems to be the following:

But if the impossibility of the 'as such' is indeed the impossibility of the 'as such',
it is also what cannot appear as such.

Derrida seems to have omitted a third alternative beyond this either/or. It is
true that death cannot appear as such. However, its *refusal to appear* or its *non-
appearance* can appear in anxiety. No doubt, the impossible is impossible. But it
does not follow that the *possibility* of the impossible is, in turn, impossible.

Heidegger is clear that, whatever else can be said of it, the possibility that
constitutes death is not a category of being. It is not a modification of presence
(see section 2). *Possibility* does not mean here unfilled actuality.

> *The closest closeness which one may have in being toward death as possibility is as
> far as possible from anything actual.* . . . Death as possibility gives Dasein nothing
> to be "actualized" and nothing that Dasein, as actual, could itself *be*. (*BT* 306–7)

Death cannot have any reality for me save as something that is to come at any
moment. The meaning of the future is determined by this imminence. But if this
future is not a modality of the present, if it cannot be thought under a category
of being as a modification of presence, then to think the relation to death is to
think, beyond being as presence, an alterity that is without common measure in
the world or without precedent in history. The uniqueness of death – of *a* death,
someone's – marks each time the end of history. It also spells the end of an entire
epoch that has sought the meaning of being by reference to the present or its
modalities.

Heidegger and Derrida are both thinkers of that end. Aware that death is not
a modality of the present, Heidegger envisages *anticipation* as a mode that puts
Dasein in relation with it, whereas Derrida sees in *mourning* (the relation with
the death of the other) a relation with a past that was never present.

Derrida's argument against Heidegger in *Aporias* must, in fact, be taken with
some caution. On the one hand, his argument suggests that the categories of
being constitute an absolute limit on thought. It is impossible to think of death,
he seems to be saying, since it cannot appear as such, that is, since it exceeds the
categories of presence or phenomenality.

But, on the other hand, Derrida's entire project of deconstruction consists
in showing that what appears as such does not constitute a limit on what can
be thought. More precisely, it consists in showing that what can appear under
a name, a concept, or an identity, does not impose a limit on what can happen.
The impossible can happen. The impossible is that for which there is (as yet) no
name, concept, or identity. *Death* in Heidegger is very much a thing like that
and, I think, Derrida knows this well.

Derrida uses the word *impossible* in at least two senses in his reading of Heidegger in *Aporias*. At times, he uses it in the classical sense to mean *that which cannot be or be conceived*. That is how he uses it when he has in mind Blanchot's claim that the instant of my death is an impossible experience. Blanchot speaks of 'the impossibility, alas, of dying' (Derrida, 1993: 77). Derrida sometimes inflects the sense of Heidegger's description of being-toward-death in that way. He says, for example, that dying is the aporia, 'the impossibility of being dead, the impossibility of living or rather "existing" one's death' (Derrida, 1993: 73). But, as François Raffoul (2010: 292) has rightly pointed out in *The Origins of Responsibility*, Heidegger's analysis of being-toward-death has nothing to do with the supposed possibility or impossibility of an experience of its occurrence.

> When Dasein dies – and even when it dies authentically – it does not have to do with an experience (*Erleben*) of its factical demising. (*BT* 291)

It is because Derrida thinks of death in Blanchot's sense as an impossible experience that, as Raffoul observes, he concludes his critical reading of Heidegger with the Levinasian claim that the death of the other is, phenomenologically, the first death.

> [I]f death is indeed the possibility of the impossible … then man, or man as *Dasein*, never has a relation to death as such, but only to perishing, to demising, and to the death of the other …. The death of the other thus becomes again 'first', always first. It is like the experience of mourning that institutes my relation to myself and constitutes the egoity of the *ego*…. The death of the other, this death of the other in 'me', is fundamentally the only death that is named in the syntagm 'my death'. (Derrida, 1993: 76)

Another sense of the *impossible* emerges in these reflections on mourning. The *impossible* here means the unique. If what constitutes *appearance* or *phenomenality* (the *as such*) is the possibility of exchange or substitution, the present or representation, identification or determination under a concept, then the unique is (the) impossible. The unique is unidentifiable against a horizon or background since it is absolutely unlike anything that was past or is present. But the impossible, Derrida insists, can be experienced. It can come to pass in mourning.

Somewhat like Ricoeur and Levinas, Derrida holds that the singularization of the *who* takes place in the ethical relation with the other human being, in friendship and mourning. As he shows in *The Politics of Friendship* and *Memoires for Paul de Man*, there is no friendship without the possibility of mourning. Since one friend must die before the other, mourning lies at the basis of friendship.

Freud conceives of mourning as labour or work, as the negation and sublation of the other into oneself, as a kind of cannibalistic process of assimilation and 'interiorization'. For Derrida (1993: 61), 'originary mourning' consists in the thoughtful remembrance (*Gedächtnis*) of the other in her singularity. It is a mourning that affirms the alterity of the other rather than a work of memory or interiorization (*Er-innerung*).

What transpires in originary mourning is the felt difference between the *memory of the other* – the other who is now nothing more than an idea or memory – and *the other's absence*, which is absolute and singular, and which the mournful self is unable to contain. That felt difference reveals the other in her uniqueness.[14] It also makes Freudian mourning impossible.

It makes what Freud calls *successful* mourning impossible where the dead other is assimilated in the self without remainder. It also makes unsuccessful mourning impossible, as Nicolas Abraham and Maria Torok describe it, where a part of the ego is identified with the dead other who then continues to live on in the ego as a stranger, unassimilated or undigested (see Derrida, 1985: 57–8).

The other who is irrevocably gone and absent draws the self to 'an absolute past' (Derrida, 1989: 66). The self cannot assimilate this past nor can it identify with it.

> Upon the death of the other we are given to memory, and thus to interiorization, since the other, outside us, is now nothing. And with the dark light of this nothing, we learn that the other resists the closure of our interiorizing memory. With the nothing of this irrevocable absence, the other appears *as* other, and as other for us, upon his death or at least in the anticipated possibility of a death. (Derrida, 1989: 34)[15]

The possibility of the friend's departure from the world is singularizing. It throws the self back on its 'terrible solitude' (Derrida, 1989: 33). It constitutes the self as a responsibility before the other, as an infinite responsibility of remembrance. Originary mourning opens the space of ethics for Derrida.

The 'other appears *as* other', he says in the passage above. The impossible can come to pass. The absolute and singular absence of the friend, which reveals the other in her uniqueness, opens itself in mourning. From that perspective, a certain rapprochement becomes possible between Heidegger and Derrida.

Derrida distinguishes originary mourning as an opening to the absolute past from the Freudian conception of mourning as labour and assimilation of the other. In a similar vein, Heidegger distinguishes anticipation as an opening to the absolute future from expectation as a relation to entities that become present in the world.

Heidegger is clear that the relation to death does not have the form of an expectation. To expect is to represent what can come to pass. Expectation puts Dasein in relation to entities with a view to their possible actualization and presence. By contrast, *vorlaufen* puts Dasein in relation with a future whose proximity to the present is infinitesimal but incalculable. Death can come at any moment. That distance between the future and the present, although miniscule, is beyond any conceivable measure. It marks the space between existence and *'the impossibility of any existence at all'* (BT 307). It is in that space of time, as we shall see in the next chapter, that Levinas's ethics of the other human being unfolds.

2

Self and Other

So we are necessarily strangers to ourselves.
—Friedrich Nietzsche, *On the Genealogy of Morals*

That voice is an order.
—Emmanuel Levinas, *The Proximity of the Other*

Es ruft mich.
—Martin Heidegger, *Being and Time*

1. Introduction

In this chapter, I extend the argument of Chapter 1, that is, that the relation to death fractures the unity of the self, into a broader problem:

- Is the alterity (of death, of time, of Dasein's being, etc.) that inhabits the self a necessary or sufficient condition for sociality?

By *sociality*, I mean the relation between the self and the other human being. In this chapter, I argue that the alterity that is interior to the self (however that alterity is conceived) is neither a necessary nor a sufficient condition to access the alterity of the other human being, that is, his or her uniqueness.

This is first shown in section 2 where I demonstrate that the central argument of Levinas's *Time and the Other* does not work. That is his claim that what is true of the relation between the present and the future of death (they cannot coincide, they are non-simultaneous, 'non-totalizable', etc.) is also true of the relation between the self and the other human being.

In section 3, I continue with Levinas with a focus on *Totality and Infinity*. He distinguishes in that text between the alterity that inhabits the self and the alterity of the other human being, and he argues that the irreducibility of the latter to the former is a necessary and sufficient condition of ethics and, by extension, of sociality.

With that understanding of ethics in mind, I show in the remainder of the chapter that some of the more recent attempts that have been made to demonstrate that we gain access to the alterity of the other via the alterity of the self must fail.

I have in mind the attempts made by Françoise Dastur in *The Call of Conscience: The Most Intimate Alterity*, François Raffoul in *The Origins of Responsibility* and Paul Ricoeur in *Oneself as Another*. These authors follow, in one way or another, Levinas's idea in *Time and the Other*, which consists in showing that the alterity that inhabits the self makes possible sociality.

Sections 4 and 5 offer a close reading of the call of conscience and guilt in *Being and Time*. They present the alterity of the self that Dastur, Raffoul and Ricoeur draw on in support of their claims.

In section 6, I show why Ricoeur's attempt to bridge the gap between Heidegger's ontological notion of guilt and Levinas's moral notion of guilt and responsibility in *Oneself as Another* does not work, and why it is not possible to derive the alterity of the other from the alterity of the self, contrary to what Dastur and Raffoul suppose.

2. Vanquishing death

In the previous chapter, I argued that the relation to death dissolves the unity of the self and that, as a result, a first-person ownership both of that relation and of one's existence before death are not possible. Does that mean that the self cannot in any way relate to its future death without dissolving in the process?

I showed in Chapter 1.6 that Derrida contends that the singularization of the *who* takes place in relation to the possible death of the friend. The other's death does not destroy the unity of the self (although I imagine that it could in some circumstances). It brings it back to its uniqueness or solitude in originary mourning. That makes possible an ethics of infinite responsibility and remembrance.

The question raised in the first paragraph above – whether the self can relate to its future death without dissolving – is one that Levinas addresses in a text published in 1947, *Time and the Other*. His treatment of that question is, appearances notwithstanding, markedly Heideggerian. Unlike Derrida and the later Levinas, for whom the death of the other is phenomenologically the first death, Levinas insists that *my* death is the first and pure figure of alterity.

The overall aim of that early text might be described negatively at first. It is a refusal to think of the relation with the other human being in terms of group identification, fusion or communion, or as participation in a common work.

Levinas wants to show that the relation between the self and the other is one of non-coincidence. To that end, he will argue as follows:

- Death is a future that will never be present. It is incommensurable with the present and its modalities. It is alterity pure and simple.
- The alterity of (the future of) death is none other than the alterity of the other human being.

That conclusion hinges on the claims that the alterity of death

(a) induces a passivity in the subject;
(b) is unknowable;
(c) both (a) and (b) are true of the alterity or uniqueness of the other human being.

It seems to follow from this that the social relation is an accomplishment of time or, what amounts to the same thing, that the non-coincidence between the future and the present makes possible the social relation.[1]

Now the social relation will be Levinas's answer to the following question:

> How can a being enter into relation with alterity without allowing its very self to be crushed by it? (Levinas, 1987: 77)

That is the problem, Levinas adds, 'of the preservation of the ego in transcendence'. He will describe it a few pages later as the problem of 'vanquishing death', and later on in the text, as 'victory over death'.

> The strangeness of the future of death does not leave the subject any initiative. There is an abyss between the present and death, between the ego and the alterity of mystery. It is not the fact that death cuts existence short, that it is end and nothingness, but the fact that the ego is absolutely without initiative in the face of it. Vanquishing death is not a problem for eternal life. Vanquishing death is to maintain, with the alterity of the event, a relation that must still be personal. (Levinas, 1987: 81)

The alterity of death does apparently not dissolve the unity of the self for Levinas.[2] Instead, it leaves it without initiative. That is because the instant of my death is absolutely 'unassumable'. It is not simply the fact that it is a limit against which the self can do nothing: light cannot be shed on it and actions cannot transform it. It is the fact that the powerlessness before that instant causes all hope to vanish and disables the ego's abilities. Before the imminence of death, Levinas (1987: 74) insists, *nous ne 'pouvons plus pouvoir'*, we are no longer 'able to be able'. That introduces a radical passivity in the subject.

What Levinas is searching for is a situation where the ego remains an ego in this state of passivity in relation to the alterity of the future. He finds it first in the erotic relation with the feminine being (the caress) and, second, in paternity, the relation with the child.

> I do not *have* my child; I *am* in some way my child. But the words 'I am' here have a significance different from an Eleatic or Platonic significance. There is a multiplicity and a transcendence in this verb 'to exist', a transcendence that is lacking in even the boldest existentialist analysis. (Levinas, 1987: 91)

The categories of power and of possession are put out of play. Neither the feminine being nor the child is owned or caused. They are both constituted by absence:

> Not absence pure and simple, not the absence of pure nothingness, but absence in a horizon of the future, an absence that is time. This is the horizon where a personal life can be constituted in the heart of the transcendent event, what I called above the 'victory over death'. (Levinas, 1987: 90)

The *victory over death* is the unfolding of a personal life between the self that exists in a state of passivity and the feminine being and the child. It is on the ground of that *victory* that Levinas will seek to prove the basic thesis of the text. This is that whatever is true of the relation between the present and the future (they cannot coincidence, they are non-totalizable, non-simultaneous, etc.) is true of the relation between the self and the other, or again that time is the relationship with the other human being.

There is doubtless something ironic and paradoxical about thinking of the social relation as something that is accomplished by *vanquishing* the undefeatable, that is, death.

The irony lies in the fact that Levinas uses the *virile* and *heroic* language – to *vanquish* or be *victorious* over death – for which he criticizes Heidegger's description of authentic existence and being-toward-death.

> Being toward death, in Heidegger's authentic existence, is a supreme lucidity and hence a supreme virility. It is *Dasein's* assumption of the uttermost possibility of

existence, which precisely makes possible all other possibilities, and consequently makes possible the very feat of grasping a possibility – that is, it makes possible activity and freedom. (Levinas, 1987: 70)

Levinas's position is somewhat reminiscent of Hegel's in *The Phenomenology of Spirit*.[3] Hegel shows that dread before death, 'the absolute master' (Hegel, 1977: 117), detaches the bondsman from his attachment to nature and to 'his natural existence'. It sets the bondsman on the path of history, that is, toward the social realization of his freedom – the realization of his being-for-self with others – in forms of mutual recognition, in the process of which this 'absolute master' is vanquished and sublated as a moment in the history of spirit.

But can death be vanquished? Is a victory over 'the absolute master' possible? Can the social relation in Levinas or Hegel attenuate or remove its corrosive effect? Far from vanquishing death, doesn't the social relation come about by foreclosing its alterity and the dread it provokes?

There seems to be a tension between what Levinas wants to think in the text and what it is possible to think. Once death is thought of as something that can be *vanquished* or over which there can be a *victory*, it is no longer *death* that one is talking about – provided that one can talk about it or that the term has a meaning, which I am not sure of (see Chapter 1.3).

Death *is* absolute alterity. Levinas is clear about this. It is the future that 'determines the future for us' (Levinas, 1987: 80). That means that death determines the meaning, essence, or form of the to-come, *l'a-venir*. It does so because it is neither present nor a modality of the present. Death constitutes the reality of time as 'the absolute impossibility of finding in the present the equivalent of the future, the lack of any hold upon the future' (Levinas, 1987: 80).

Accordingly, the future of death cannot be assumed, let alone vanquished, if *to assume* and *vanquish* are modes of the present, or what amounts to the same thing, abilities of the ego. To *vanquish* death, whatever else that might mean, would be to close the interval of time that separates this moment from my death. But a meaningful life with the other, *sociality*, is possible thanks to the fact that there is still time, that my death postpones itself, that the distance between now and then, although infinitesimal, has not yet closed.

If vanquishing death is impossible, if, beyond merely disabling the ego's abilities, death fractures its unity and dissolves it, then we stand facing a dilemma.

(a) Either the self must dissolve in the encounter with the other human being, contrary to what Levinas expects and hopes, since the alterity of the other human being is the living figure and presence of the alterity of death.

(b) Or the relation between the present and the future of death cannot be
     identical with the relation between the self and the other human being, or
     again what is true of the former cannot be true of the latter.

It is probably because of some of these difficulties and tensions in this early text
that Levinas came to rethink the encounter with the other human being in terms
of the *trace* or the absolute past.

3. Alterity

Levinas, I believe, fails to think the social relation in this early work in terms of
the alterity of death that inhabits the self. That failure is instructive. It shows,
among other things, the equally hazardous and, I think, not very successful
attempts that have more recently been made by some Heidegger scholars and
other authors to think the social relation in more or less the same way as Levinas
does in *Time and the Other*, notably, on the basis of an alterity that inhabits
the self.

I have in mind scholars who have argued that Heidegger's thinking of being,
both early and late, is an insistent meditation on alterity, more precisely, on the
alterity of the self in the call of conscience and the alterity of being in relation to
beings, and that this thought is, consequently, already ethical.

That line of argument has been pursued by Françoise Dastur in *The Call of
Conscience: The Most Intimate Alterity*, by François Raffoul in *The Origins of
Responsibility* and by Paul Ricoeur in the tenth and final study of *Oneself as
Another*.

These authors focus on Heidegger's analysis of conscience in *Being and Time*,
which makes evident the fact that the self is structured by an inner alterity or
foreignness. They infer from this fact that the existential analytic comprises an
ethical dimension that is close, if not identical, to Levinas's ethics in *Totality and
Infinity*, since the alterity of conscience is what gives the self an access to the
other human being.

None of these authors contests that there is a difference between the alterity
that inhabits the self, which is originary or non-derivable, not reducible to the
internalization of the other as in Freud's superego, and the alterity of the other
human being. But they argue that the experience of the first is a condition of
possibility of gaining access to the second – that the alterity of the other human
being reveals itself in the alterity of conscience.

There are several reasons why I have failed to be convinced by that argument. In the first place, the difference between the alterity of conscience and the alterity of the other is, as Ricoeur himself acknowledges (see section 6), *irreducible*. That puts pressure on the idea that we can say with good phenomenological reason that the first gives *access* to the second.

Second, we might say, from Levinas's perspective, that it is this irreducible difference that opens the abyss between ontology or existential analysis, on the one hand, and, on the other, ethics properly so-called. Why *properly so-called*?

Because nothing less than the alterity of the other, his uniqueness, unmediated or undiluted by the alterity of conscience, can summon the subject to an *unconditional* responsibility. Anything less than that would situate ethics in the political or economic context of a relation of reciprocity and exchange between the self and the other, of debt and the imputation of debt, of obligations contracted and discharged.

Lastly, Levinas himself, not so much in what he says as in his choice of words, warns us against this gesture of *deriving* the second from the first type of alterity. He thinks of alterity in two quite different ways in *Totality and Infinity*, as an alterity that inhabits the self and as the alterity of the other human being. The first is described by means of the Cartesian *idea of infinity*, which is immanent to the *cogito*, and the second by means of *the face*.

The idea of infinity that overflows the self who thinks it is an alterity at the heart of the self. It is its possibility of being otherwise than self-interested. The whole of *Totality and Infinity* revolves around the idea that the presence of the other in speech, exposure to the uprightness of his face, is necessary to produce the idea of infinity in me. That is not the production of the other but of a subjectivity that is for-the-other, of a disinterested desire.

As Levinas says at the start of *Totality and Infinity*, 'the deformalization or the concretization of the idea of infinity' is produced as desire. But desire 'presuppose[s] a relationship in which the Desirable arrests the "negativity" of the I'. It presupposes an encounter with the face, 'presence before a face' (Levinas, 1979: 50).

The other exceeds the idea I have of him. That excess is what produces the idea of infinity in me. And that idea is what radically transforms my subjectivity. Hospitality, a subjectivity that welcomes the other, rather than self-interest, a subject that adheres to its being, consummates the idea of infinity (Levinas, 1979: 27). The irreducibility of the alterity of the other human being to the alterity of the self is just what makes it possible for there to be an ethical subject.

I think that Levinas is right about this. There is an unbridgeable gap between taking as one's point of orientation, in the analysis of human existence, one of these two possibilities:

(a) The possibility of being affected by the alterity that inhabits the self (as conceived in Heidegger, not in Freud or Nietzsche or Michel Henry, etc.).
(b) The possibility of being affected by the alterity of the other human being (as conceived in Levinas).

Dastur and Raffoul want to derive (b) from (a), which doesn't work, whereas Ricoeur proposes a hybridization of both positions, which produces consequences that he does not seem to anticipate.

Let me begin by exploring the first point of orientation (a) in *Being and Time*.

4. The call

Attestation, testimony, evidence. That is the principal theme of chapter 2 of Division II of *Being and Time* titled 'Dasein's attestation of an authentic potentiality-for-being, and resoluteness.' Following section 53, which concludes with a description of Dasein's anticipation of death as authentic possibility, chapter 2 stages an encounter of Dasein with itself, an encounter that takes the form of a bearing witness to self. Dasein is to give an ontical attestation of an ontological possibility. That means that the call of conscience and resoluteness, which accomplish that attestation, will bring Dasein in direct contact with its being, and that the relation between the ontological and the ontic, between Dasein *qua* 'actual' entity (*BT* 307) and its being *qua* thrown projection, is not of the order of a seeing or reflecting. It is a relation of call and response, a bearing witness and readiness to action.

The attestation of the ontological by the ontic gives priority to the voice and tonality (*Stimme, Stimmung*) over the ability to see or reflect. That is why the existential analytic has from the start a practical dimension – why *theoria*, the thinking of being, is also at once a *praxis* that calls the thinker to be otherwise, to be itself authentically, that is, to be responsible for its being. It is the highest *praxis*, Heidegger will specify at the start of the *Letter on Humanism* (*BW* 217).

That attestation is not an achievement of the phenomenologist *per se*. At any rate, its initiating source does not lie in the phenomenologist. Dasein 'demands (*fordert*) this of itself' (*BT* 311). The phenomenologist follows this call. She submits to this demand. She follows its lead by making explicit its content and direction, that is to say, by moving against the flow of Dasein's falling tendency.

It is as if Dasein's being called for a bearing witness to itself, as if its being exhausted itself in this calling forth and making-itself-evident in being heard, and the ontic attestation was nothing other than the resolute response, a transformative and genuine hearing. That is where the poverty or finitude of the ontological becomes acutely visible.

Being is manifest to Dasein as a voice whose silence calls it forth to be itself authentically. It solicits a response, an ontic attestation, a change in the world. The ontological is the chance for introducing something new in the world. It is *praxis*.

Heidegger explains his heterodox approach to conscience in section 54 and sums up the conclusions he aims to arrive at by the end of the chapter. Conscience is not to be taken as an oracle in the soul issuing commands and prohibitions, as a voice in the psyche that admonishes and approves its bad and good intentions or deeds or as a product of the evolution of the species with a pragmatic value. The ontological analysis of conscience takes place on this side of all anthropology, psychology, biology and theology. It is an analysis of conscience *beyond good and evil*.

The aim of the analysis is to expose conscience as a phenomenon of Dasein, a phenomenon in which Dasein is responsive to its being. Heidegger will argue that the call of conscience calls Dasein to its ownmost self, that it does so by summoning it to its guilt, and that the mode of hearing the call, of responding to the call of guilt, is '*wanting to have a conscience*' (*BT* 314). To properly listen to the call will amount to making a choice, choosing to be guilty.

That is why inauthenticity is, in the final analysis, a failure to hear (*hören*), a failure to belong (*gehören*), a failure to choose and be decisive (*Entscheidung*). It is an irresponsible, vacillating because not an explicitly owned, self-chosen life, an existence that avoids the moment of *krisis* by avoiding to go to the limit of what it can be. *Das Man* 'deprives the particular Dasein of its responsibility' and decisions by making itself answerable for everything (*BT* 165).

> Losing itself in the publicness and the idle talk of the 'they', it fails to hear its own Self in listening to the they-self. If Dasein is to be able to get brought back from this lostness of failing to hear itself, and if this is to be done through itself, then it must first be able to find itself – to find itself as something which has failed to hear itself, and which fails to hear in that it listens away to the 'they'. This listening-away must be broken off (*gebrochen*); in other words, the possibility of another kind of hearing which will interrupt it, must be given by Dasein itself. (*BT* 315–16)

To be authentic does not mean to listen to oneself as opposed to listening to others. This listening-away, inauthenticity, must be broken and breached; it must be pierced by another kind of voice than the one heard in mundane speech. Authenticity is a leap, a break in discourse. It is a crisis brought on by the call of conscience. Deafened by the idle chatter of public discourse in which Dasein talks of its everyday affairs with entities and others, it is solicited by a call to turn its ear from entities or others in the world to their being and, first and foremost, to its being-in-the-world. The call 'arouses another kind of hearing, which, in relationship to the hearing that is lost, has a character in every way opposite' (*BT* 316). To be authentic is to be oneself self-responsibly. This becomes possible once Dasein finds itself attuned to the anxiety of being-in-the-world and hears what is silently accomplished by it, the disclosure of being-in-the-world.

The groundlessness and idleness of mundane discourse could not be arrested, it could not be brought to a halt, save by an essential silence. The voice of conscience does not express itself in verbal utterances. It does not speak. Or rather, it speaks by not speaking. Heidegger dissociates the voice (*Stimme*) from the mouth, the phonetic apparatus of man, and associates it with the understanding. The ' "voice" is taken rather as a giving-to-understand (*Zu-verstehen-geben*)' (*BT* 316). This *call* or *voice* is not a metaphor, a trope or manner of speaking, as Ricoeur believes (1992: 341). It is to be taken literally as a discursive event that is experienced as a 'push' (*Stoßes*), as an 'abrupt arousal' (*Aufrüttelns*), or as an awakening or being summoned.

Speech for Heidegger is a mode of disclosure. To speak is to say something about something. It is to make it manifest as this or as that. That is why the voice that speaks by keeping silent brings Dasein back to itself, why it discloses Dasein as a discursive site of disclosure. This essential silence is not a privation of speech, being dumb. It is a redoubled speech, something akin to writing perhaps. It is like a discourse that calls its own mode of being into question, what Paul de Man calls *literature*.

Conscience calls Dasein *to* become itself authentically and calls it back *from* the inauthenticity of its lostness in the public world of *das Man*. The unidirectionality of the call, this *from-to* relation, cannot be mapped onto the 'vertical' (Ricoeur, 1992: 342) relation between the caller and the called. The caller is neither the one nor the other, Dasein in its authenticity or inauthenticity. It is Dasein in its pure facticity, disclosed to itself in anxiety before death as being there pure and simple.

> If the caller is asked about its name (*Namen*), status (*Stand*), origin, descent (*Herkunft*), or repute (*Ansehen*), it not only refuses to answer, but does not even

leave the slightest possibility of one's making it into something with which we can be familiar when one's understanding of Dasein has a 'worldly' orientation. [The caller] holds itself aloof from any way of becoming well known, and this belongs to its phenomenal character.

This refusal to make itself known and familiar, 'the indefiniteness and indeterminacy of the caller (*Unbestimmtheit und Unbestimmbarkeit des Rufers*)', makes known 'that the caller is solely absorbed in summoning us to something' (*BT* 319).

But can we then be certain that the author of the call is Dasein in its pure facticity? Must we follow Heidegger in that regard?

The caller has all the characteristics of an absolute stranger, that is, of a being that has been stripped of all characteristics. It is a being that is unidentifiable by name, gender, race, status, provenance or birth. It is a being that is without identity or identifying attributes, a stranger whose mode of being consists strictly in calling, summoning or appealing (*Aufruf*), and whose silence betrays, perhaps, a weakness, a vulnerability that unsettles the familiarity of the at-home, much like the unnamed wanderer in George Trakl's poem, *A Winter Evening*, whose 'pain has turned the threshold' of the home 'to stone' (*PLT* 205).

The call of conscience does not summon Dasein as a member of a particular identity group, whether racial, gender or national. More generally, it does not summon Dasein as an instance of a kind, since the call would then aim at Dasein as a being that is replaceable by other instances of the same kind. Just as there is no such thing as 'death in general' (*HCT* 313), so there is no such thing as a *general call* or *call in general* aiming at a plurality, a people or a mass. Or if such calls do transpire in the public world of *das Man*, then they must be inauthentic modifications of the call of conscience that singles out Dasein in its irreplaceability.

To be the recipient of a call or address, of a summons, is to have been singled out as this one and no other. It is impossible not to respond to a summons: turning away or ignoring it, whether deliberately or involuntarily, is a definite and unequivocal response. It is above all impossible for anyone to take my place in fulfilling my responsibility to respond to the call.

A call that singles me out heightens the non-replaceability of my existence. It highlights the fact that my responsibility to respond is non-transferrable, that it is in each case mine.

The call elects me in the nakedness of my existence as an ipseity. It passes over (*übergeht*) my worldly identities as if they had become entirely meaningless. The call brings them to naught (*Bedeutungslosigkeit*) (*BT* 317). It brings to naught everything that contributes to my being at home in the world, everything that endows my surroundings, my past and my future, my relationships with others, with a sense of familiarity, particularly my membership to a certain gender, race, nation, culture, tradition and history. The call constrains me to return to and understand my existence as a sensibility, a passivity, a being-responsive to the strangeness of a silent call or, perhaps, to the silent call of a stranger.

The caller who summons me is not localizable in a determinate place in history or space. Is the caller *inside* or *outside* of me? Dasein cannot determine where the caller is. It cannot identify the source of the call, its author.

Gerufen wird aus der Ferne in die Ferne.

'The call is from afar unto afar', Heidegger says (*BT* 316). None of the spatial terms usually used to identify things and events in the world – *inside, outside, where, far, here, there* – can be assigned a determinate reference in the case of the call. It is as if the caller had dis-identified itself with a place of origin (*Herkunft*), had not yet or already crossed the threshold of Dasein's home or world, is in effect nothing other than this pure passage or transition across borders and thresholds.

That is why the call strikes Dasein with an unheard-of strangeness and unfamiliarity, and why the call is for the most part avoided. *To avoid* here is to not hear what one hears. It seems that, in evading the call, Dasein causes the very thing it wants to avoid to return. Turning away from the call does not obliterate it. It provokes its unhomely return and testifies to its inescapability.

If the author of the call is indefinite and indeterminate, as Heidegger acknowledges, then we have nothing by way of distinguishing it from the call. We cannot distinguish the *caller* from the *call* as we distinguish an agent from the action it performs, or as we distinguish a *cause* from its *effect*. *Agent* and *action* here seem to be one and the same. What occupies the place of the grammatical subject in the sentence *it calls* is not a self or ego. It is the verb *calling*. There is here no *doer* behind the *deed*. We could say, following Nietzsche (1989: 45), that 'the deed is everything'.

There is no measure to the silence through which the call summons Dasein. It exceeds the limits of mundane speech. It arrests its groundlessness, and affects Dasein beyond its calculations, beyond the calculations of its will and the horizon of its expectations.

> The call is precisely something which we ourselves have neither planned nor prepared for nor voluntarily performed, nor have we ever done so. '*Es*' *ruft*, 'it' calls, against our expectations and even against our will. (*BT* 320)

Since the caller for Heidegger is Dasein in its pure facticity, the strangeness of the voice is evidence for him that the self is structured by an inner alterity or by a transcendence in immanence, as Husserl might say.

The 'call undoubtedly does not come from someone else who is with me in the world'.

*Der Ruf kommt **aus** mir und doch **über** mich.*

That suggests at least two possible translations. The call comes *from* me and yet from *beyond* me. The call that comes *from* me nevertheless *overwhelms* me.

The feeling of unfamiliarity that overwhelms Dasein when it is affected by the call of conscience is, in the final analysis for Heidegger, a response to the temporalization of ecstatic temporality. The *it* that calls is the *it* that gives being to be understood as presence (see *BT* 255). It is what accomplishes the disclosure of Dasein in anxiety. The call of conscience is care as the call of time.

Heidegger will describe the call as 'like an *alien, foreign* voice', a *fremde Stimme* (*BT* 321). Contrary to what Derrida (1991: 110) and Courtine (1991: 87) suppose, this foreign voice is not identical with 'the voice of the friend (*der Stimme des Freundes*) whom every Dasein carries with it' (*BT* 206). Unless the friend can play the role of an alien or foreign voice that speaks by not speaking, which Heidegger's text does not seem to rule out.

At any rate, the foreign voice in the self is, for Heidegger, originary and non-derivable. It does not issue from the alterity of the other Dasein. It is not the internalization of the other Dasein in the form of a moral conscience or superego. The *it* that calls is neither God nor a person with authority or power, an ancestor. Nor can this voice be explained biologically. What is obliterated when the voice is interpreted theologically, anthropologically or biologically is the phenomenal finding. That is the abrupt arousal, the push or jolt, the surprise that is solicited by the call owing to its foreignness to everything known and familiar.

But if what constitutes the phenomenal finding of the voice is its sheer unfamiliarity, this absolute non-knowing of what or who speaks by keeping silent, then how can Heidegger be sure that the caller *is* Dasein in its pure facticity?

What if this Dasein, which finds itself in the very depths of its uncanniness, should be the caller of the call of conscience? (*BT* 321)

Isn't Heidegger transgressing the phenomenal findings the moment he identifies the voice with Dasein?

Is there a better reason for saying that the caller is Dasein than that it is the face of the other, which also calls 'in its silence' (Bernasconi and Wood, 2003: 169) and which is also entirely foreign? Given the terms in which Heidegger has framed the caller at the start of section 57, it cannot be ruled out. It does not seem to be possible to decide who the caller is, whether it is the alterity of the self or the alterity of the other.

Can *Dasein* in its authenticity resolve that question and decide who the caller is when the caller is manifest in discourse by its silence and when it is present in the neutrality and impersonality of the *it*? The distinction between the *who* and the *what*, first introduced at the start of *Being and Time* in order to distinguish between the ipseity of Dasein and entities other than Dasein, appears to be no longer of any pertinence here.

The problem comes to a head in the latter part of section 57 where Heidegger continuously slides from the impersonal *it* to the *self* of Dasein. In its *who*, he says, the caller is definable in a 'worldly' way by *nothing* at all. It is unfamiliar to the everyday they-self. He then wonders:

> What could be more alien to the 'they', lost in the manifold 'world' of its concern, than the Self which has been singularized down to itself in uncanniness and been thrown into the 'nothing'? 'It' calls ... (*BT* 321–2)

We must ask whether this sliding from the *it* to the *self* compromises the ontological rigor of the analysis of conscience in *Being and Time*, whether it announces a slide into an ontical analysis, of an anthropological or psychological nature perhaps.

If the caller is at bottom the *being* of Dasein, as it undoubtedly is for Heidegger – that is, temporality in the neutrality and impersonality of its temporalization – then the difference between the ontological and the ontic must find itself imperiled once the caller is identified with Dasein's proper self (*eigene Selbst*), its ontic singularity, the same self to which Dasein is summoned by the caller (*BT* 317).

This danger is perhaps not surprising, although avoidable, in a context where ontology, as in Heidegger's *Being and Time*, has an irreducible practical and existential dimension, that is, given that the being of beings understood as their disclosure is always also the event of questioning being and of being put into question by it in the ipseity of one's existence.

5. Guilt

What Ricoeur finds problematic in Heidegger's analysis of conscience is not the ambiguity affecting its ontological status, nor Heidegger's decision to identify the caller with Dasein in its pure facticity: It is its status of being beyond morality.

Heidegger's is an analysis of conscience that neutralizes the moral demand imposed by the other on the self. Ricoeur notes that 'cut off from the demands of others and from any properly moral determination, resoluteness remains just as indeterminate as the call to which it seems to reply'.

> To this demoralization of conscience, I would oppose a conception that closely associates the phenomenon of *injunction* to that of *attestation*. (Ricoeur, 1992: 350–1)

Attestation for Ricoeur is not the ontic vindication of an ontological possibility. It is the auto-affection experienced in the call of conscience.

Conscience is the structure of selfhood. It gives itself something to understand. It attests to its being guilty or indebted. Instead of teasing out the meaning of *Sein* in *Schuldig-sein*, as Heidegger does in section 58 of *Being and Time*, Ricoeur focuses on the meaning of *Schuld*. Conscience instructs the self that it is guilty in the second person, *you*, rather than in the first person where the emphatic *Guilty!* turns up as a predicate of the *I am* (BT 326).

That injunction suggests that the auto-affection of conscience cannot be distinguished from a being-affected-by-the-other since only the other would address me in the second person. The self-affection of conscience is then a modality of hetero-affection. This reorients the direction and sense of debt or responsibility away from the self and toward the other, and it adds to the analysis of conscience the ethical dimension that, in Ricoeur's eyes, is missing in Heidegger.

> Being-enjoined would then constitute the moment of otherness proper to the phenomenon of conscience, in accordance with the metaphor of the voice. Listening to the voice of conscience would signify being-enjoined by the Other. In this way, the rightful place of the notion of *debt* would be acknowledged, a notion that was too hastily ontologized by Heidegger at the expense of the ethical dimension of indebtedness. (Ricoeur, 1992: 351)

Ricoeur's hermeneutics of conscience aims to find a middle ground between what he perceives to be two extreme and undesirable lines of thought: on the one hand, Heidegger's ontological notion of guilt, which issues from the alterity of the self, and, on the other, Levinas's moral notion of guilt or responsibility, which issues from the alterity of the other. What Ricoeur invites us to reflect on is a moral sense of guilt that comes from the alterity of the self and that gives it access to the other.

Let me start with Heidegger. Heidegger highlights two ordinary senses of guilt in his analysis of what conscience gives Dasein to understand in section 58. The first sense is *owing something to someone*. The second is *being responsible for something*, that is, *being the author* or *cause of something*. Combined together, Heidegger contends that *guilt* ordinarily signifies *making oneself responsible by incurring a debt*.

Formalizing this ordinary sense, Heidegger draws from it the idea of *Grundsein einer Nichtigkeit, being responsible for a not* or *being the ground of a nullity* (*BT* 329).[4] This formal-existential notion comes into effect with the anticipation of death.

The possibility of death – the fact that the world will, at some time, have nothing more to say to me, that I will have departed from the world – throws Dasein back on its existence pure and simple. That constrains Dasein to choose how it must live its existence: Either it must continue living it as *one* lives it, and understand itself from what it does or it must assume responsibility for it as its irreplaceable possibility. That is a choice that haunts Dasein every moment.

In choosing itself, Dasein resolves to repeat choosing itself in every factical situation. To resolve on that is to want to have a conscience (*Gewissen-haben-wollen*). It is to choose being guilty (*BT* 334). That choice is the condition for action. What does it mean to be guilty here?

I am guilty not because of what I have done, say, because I have committed a crime or because I have failed in my moral duty. Guilt or responsibility precedes freedom and action. I am guilty not because I am not the ground of my existence but, rather, because I am given over to it from the start. I am guilty because I rest in the weight of a projection that I have not accomplished and that is nevertheless mine to accomplish each time.

There is no sense of the *ought* (*Sollen*) here. Heidegger is not saying that I ought to have accomplished that projection but that I am guilty since I haven't done so. Guilt must 'be detached from relationship to any law or "ought"' (*BT* 328).

To be guilty or to be the ground of a nullity is a value-neutral existential. It picks out an ontological condition of Dasein. That is that it is affected by its existence. It is passive with respect to it. It is as if the first projection in which Dasein first appeared to itself was accomplished in an irreversible past beyond recall, as if every subsequent projection it accomplished as its own rested on that past that it cannot retrieve, resume or assume as its *own* and that it had, in consequence, to endure it as something that is foreign to it – that is, as something that is foreign to its freedom and into which, therefore, it has been irreducibly *thrown*.

Choosing to be guilty, or resolving to repeat choosing itself, is, I think, Dasein's access to that immemorial past. That is how Dasein intensifies the burden of its existence, namely, by bringing to life, in the moment, this past that is both foreign and proper to it. Anticipatory resoluteness intensifies Dasein's existence and prepares it for action. It makes present its factical situation in the horizon of that immemorial past and imminent death.

For Ricoeur (1992: 355), however, whose aim is to rehabilitate a moral sense of guilt, this analysis is insufficient. Unless Dasein's attestation of its guilt or passivity is also an injunction from the other, it 'risks losing all ethical or moral significance'.

On the other hand, Ricoeur (1992: 337) criticises Levinas's 'hyperbolic' description of the self as existing in total separation, as sheer concern for self in enjoyment, as interested in persevering in its being and, conjointly with this, of the other as absolute exteriority.

The ethical relation for Levinas is instituted by the alterity of the other, his uniqueness, which interrupts separation by soliciting the interested self to be disinterested. It constitutes a subjectivity that issues in giving, generosity, or hospitality, at the limit, a giving of one's self and of one's world to the other without reserve, a generosity without reciprocity or the expectation of return, a hospitality where the host, the master of the house, is at once a guest and the guest a host, and the home a place of refuge or exile for both – a subjectivity, in short, that is from top to bottom a being-for-the-other.

What summons the self to this infinite responsibility is the uprightness of the other's face, its nakedness. Whatever demeanour or masks it puts on, the face cannot hide the other's vulnerability and exposure to death, a vulnerability that at once tempts the self to liquidate the other – weakness is always an invitation to violence – and commands the self to not kill him, instructs it to not leave the other die alone (but with an authority that does not humiliate the self, that is without force or power).

Ricoeur believes that this absolute dissymmetry between the self and the other is excessive. The injunction from the other must at the same time be a self-attestation of conscience. Otherwise 'the injunction risks not being heard and the self not being affected in the mode of being-enjoined'.

Ricoeur thus claims that conscience, understood as an injunction-attestation, a mode of hetero-affection that structures selfhood, shows up as a third modality of alterity, one that is irreducible to the ontological alterity of the self (Heidegger) and the ethical alterity of the other (Levinas).

To these alternatives – either Heidegger's strange(r)ness or Levinas' externality –
I shall stubbornly oppose the original and originary character of what appears
to me to constitute the third modality of otherness, namely *being enjoined as the
structure of selfhood.* (Ricoeur, 1992: 354)

6. Responsibility

The danger that Ricoeur exposes himself to is that, in refusing to subscribe to the
rigors of an ontological analysis, his hermeneutics of conscience opens itself to
an anthropological or theological reading, and, in its refusal to assign a priority
of meaning to the alterity of the other, the encounter with the other falls short of
the ethical force he expects it to have on the self.

This danger arises largely as a result of the fact that he apparently makes no
use of the transcendence of conscience he yet clearly spells out.

> Unlike the dialogue of the soul with itself, of which Plato speaks, this affection by
> another voice presents a remarkable dissymmetry, one that can be called vertical,
> between the agency that calls and the self called upon. It is the vertical nature
> of the call, equal to its interiority, that creates the enigma of the phenomenon of
> conscience. (Ricoeur, 1992: 342)

This vertical relation experienced in conscience testifies to its transcendence,
which is open to two readings, as ontological or as ethical transcendence.

It can be read, as Heidegger does, as a vertical relation between the ontological
and the ontic, as a relation of call and response. Transcendence designates here
the ontical attestation of an ontological possibility called for by Dasein itself. It is
a relation in which the self is constituted as a being guilty, a passivity or response
to the strangeness of a silent call that singles it out each time, whether or not it
owns up to the fact that it has been summoned.

It can also be read, as Levinas does in *Nonintentional Consciousness* and
From the One to the Other, as a vertical relation between the self and the other,
where the self exists in a state of passivity and is exposed to the other, a state that
Levinas calls 'bad conscience'.

> Bad conscience or timidity: accused without culpability and responsible for its
> very presence. Reserve of the non-invested, the non-justified, the 'stranger on
> the earth', in the words of the Psalmist, the stateless or homeless person, who
> dares not enter.

'The interiority of the mental', he suggests, 'is perhaps originally this' (Levinas, 1998: 129).

The bad conscience for Levinas is not an internal moral agency that admonishes the self for its misdeeds, that loads it with guilt for its forbidden wishes or that monitors, checks and disciplines the self's outward behaviour. It is a rethinking of the pre-reflexive *cogito* in phenomenology.

Levinas rightly prefers to call the consciousness that accompanies the consciousness of the world *non-reflexive* or *non-intentional* instead of *pre-reflexive*. In the first place, the latter term misleadingly suggests that this consciousness has the latent theoretical aim of turning itself into an object of reflection and knowledge. Second, this accompanying consciousness is, in its passivity, already exposed to the other, and the direction to the other is not instituted by consciousness in a *noesis* or act of meaning, that is, autonomously. It is instituted by the other, that is, heteronomously.

Levinas calls that consciousness 'stateless' or 'homeless' because it has none of the identifying attributes the ego ascribes to itself. It is a non-egological consciousness, without an immanent unifying centre, much like Sartre's impersonal consciousness in *Transcendence and the Ego*.

> The noninentional is passivity from the start, and the accusative is in a sense its 'first case'. (Levinas, 1998: 144)

The passivity of the self is the consciousness of being put into question by the other. It is the fear for the violence the *I* or ego may do to the other. It is the timidity with regard to its very presence, which risks putting the other in exile. As if 'the principle of identity positing itself triumphantly as *I* carried with it an indecency and violence, as if the *I* prohibited, by its very positing, the full existence of the other' (Levinas, 1998: 165).

What we find in the deepest recesses of the mind, Levinas is saying, in the consciousness that accompanies the consciousness of the world, is not the self-constituting flow of inner-time consciousness but an exposure to the other human being. The self is in its passivity constituted as a responsibility without measure.

The route to the other, then, is not by way of the interiority of the soul, as if the soul was at first inside itself and then, upon falling into space, the body or history found its way outside. The relation of self-to-self in the dialogue of the soul with itself presupposes sociality. It is a 'forgotten sociality' (Levinas, 1998: 163).

Ricoeur, who wants to bypass the perceived excesses in Heidegger and Levinas – the ontological notion of guilt, the exteriority of the other – understands the vertical relation exhibited by the call of conscience as the index of an alterity that is immanent to the structure of selfhood and that is manifest in the phenomenon of injunction, in being-enjoined in the second person, which gives *guilt* an ethical sense. But he appears to believe that that is sufficient to think of the self in more or less the same way as Levinas, namely, as a self that is constituted in its ipseity as an infinite responsibility for the other.

The difficulty appears in Ricoeur's text when, like Heidegger, he is concerned to identify who the caller is, the source of the injunction. Unlike Heidegger, for whom the caller is the being of Dasein, Ricoeur, who has taken leave of ontology, is constrained to identify the source of the injunction with the anthropological or theological other.

Ricoeur subscribes to the ambiguity of the closing chapter of Spirit in Hegel's *Phenomenology of Spirit* titled *Conscience. The 'beautiful soul', evil and its forgiveness*. In this chapter, it remains unclear whether the 'reconciling *Yea*' (Hegel, 1977: 409) in which the judging and acting consciousnesses recognize each other as recognizing their finitude and partiality issues from the voice of Spirit or of God, whether it is the word of the anthropological or the theological other.

> The ultimate equivocalness with respect to the status of the Other in the phenomenon of conscience is perhaps what needs to be preserved in the final analysis. (Ricoeur, 1992: 353)

But can it be preserved? Is it possible to leave undecided who the caller is? Does it not make a difference to what I *owe* the other whether the other is the theological other or, conversely, the anthropological other? Is my debt to God qualitatively the same as my debt to the other human being?

Perhaps it is. It is, at any rate, for Levinas. And it also appears to be for Ricoeur, who shares 'Levinas' conviction that the other is the necessary path of injunction' (Ricoeur, 1992: 355), and who, in addition, commits himself to the idea of justice as 'an infinite *mutual indebtedness*, which is not without recalling Levinas' theme of the hostage' (Ricoeur, 1992: 202). Ricoeur wants to say that my debt to the other is infinite or unconditional. That is how he rediscovers the dissymmetry that resides at the heart of conscience in the social relation between the self and the other, whilst reserving a place for 'self-esteem' as a 'figure of recognition' (Ricoeur, 1992: 331), absent in Levinas.

Ricoeur writes at the end of *Oneself as Another* that we cannot know who the source of the injunction is, whether it is 'another person whom I can look in the face or who can stare at me, or my ancestors for whom there is no representation, to so great an extent does my debt to them constitute my very self, or God – living God, absent God – or an empty place'.

But do I not know who the source of the injunction is? Do I not know that the caller is *neither the theological nor the anthropological other*?

Ricoeur is right when he insists a few sentences above that 'the otherness of conscience is to be held irreducible to that of other people' (Ricoeur, 1992: 355). There is *no* phenomenological or hermeneutic justification for *transposing* the vertical relation that structures the interiority of the self *onto* the social relation between the self and the other (something that Ricoeur apparently thinks we can do with good reason). In the final analysis, I know who the source of the injunction is. It is my conscience that enjoins me in the second person that I am indebted to the other. I assign myself that responsibility towards the other in the hetero-affective experience of conscience. Since it is authored and conditioned by nothing other than myself, it issues from an act of freedom.

That self-authored responsibility also fits closely the ethico-political doctrine of *Oneself as Another*. That is the doctrine that one must 'recognize oneself as being enjoined *to live well with and for others in just institutions and to esteem oneself as the bearer of this wish*' (Ricoeur, 1992: 352).

If it is true that the alterity of conscience is *irreducible* to the alterity of the other, then that is also true of the injunction of conscience in relation to the injunction of the other. I simply cannot see how it is possible to identify the injunction of the other, whether God or the other human being, with the injunction of conscience, even when the latter is voiced in the second person. But it is the injunction of the other that places me under an ethical responsibility. Hence the hetero-affection of conscience is not a sufficient condition of ethics (at least in the Levinasian sense of that term).

Françoise Dastur and François Raffoul are no doubt right to emphasize that the alterity of conscience, the experience of passivity in being enjoined in the second person, opens the self to the other. But they want to say more than that. They insist that the alterity of conscience makes apparent not merely the other, but the other in his or her alterity or uniqueness.

The alterity of the other is revealed in the alterity of conscience, and takes place in the alteration of the self. (Raffoul, 2010: 208)

Or as Dastur writes,

> The alterity of the Other appears within the alterity of conscience. (Dastur, 2002: 95)

We have seen in section 2 that Levinas's attempt to reach the same conclusion in *Time and the Other* failed. Even if we accept the claim that the alterity that inhabits the self opens it to the other human being and makes possible the social relation – which is in any case doubtful, as David Wood (2005: 65; see fn. 1) convincingly shows – it is still not clear why that transcendence in immanence, that interior difference, should disclose the uniqueness of the *other* rather than the uniqueness of the *self*.

Ricoeur seems to be closer to the truth when he says that conscience gives access to an indeterminate plurality, 'other people'.

> The otherness of the Other is then the counterpart ... to this passivity specific to being-enjoined. Now, what more is there to say about the otherness of this Other? ... is not this Other, in one way or another, other people?

Ricoeur cannot maintain at the same time that the source of the injunction is equivocal – it could be the anthropological *or* the theological other – and that the source of the injunction is the other in his incomparable uniqueness, my beloved. The 'uniqueness of the unique is the uniqueness of the beloved. The uniqueness of the unique *signifies* in love' (Levinas, 1998: 167). My beloved is irreplaceable, and his irreplaceability makes the source of the injunction – the point in the universe that orients my entire being and on which my infinite responsibility is focused – unequivocal.

If the alterity of conscience highlights the singularity of my existence, as Heidegger shows, it remains irreducible to the singularity of the other, as Ricoeur teaches. But it is from the singularity of the other, manifest in love or in the vulnerability of his face, that the ethical relation, the relation of infinite responsibility, derives its meaning.

Figurations

1. Introduction

It is clear from the previous two chapters that the relation to death (Chapter 1) and sociality (Chapter 2) are akin in some respect. They are accomplished in different ways as a relation with a future that is discontinuous with the present. Death is, like the singularity of the other human being, something that will never be present. Or more precisely, it is something that will never be present to me save as an irreducible and originary absence in my world. In this chapter, I show that *hospitality* accomplishes a relation with a future in that sense, too.

The main argument of this chapter can be summed up as follows:

- Being (the event of appearing) is unthinkable otherwise than as a figuration of someone or something or, more precisely, as a figure in which the distinction between the *who* and the *what* has become fuzzy and unstable.
- Such a figure is without a determinable identity, that is, it is a figure of the future.
- The relation with the future is made concrete as hospitality.

In section 2, I begin by showing that what Levinas calls *ontology* and Heidegger *metaphysics* share a family resemblance. My aim is to explain, in the background of that resemblance, the reason why they diverge in their thinking of absolute alterity.

I address David Wood's objection to Levinas's understanding of absolute alterity in *The Step Back: Ethics and Politics after Deconstruction*: that is that Levinas unduly restricts it to the other human being. Building on Wood's objection, I argue that some conditions must be met if an event is to be worthy of the name. One of these conditions is that it must be an origin of meaning or a source of phenomenalization, and I show that this condition cannot be satisfied unless it is a figuration of being.

To make that claim concrete, I turn in section 3 to the feminine in Levinas and, in section 4, to the absolute *arrivant* in Derrida, to show in what way they are both figurations of being.

2. Proximities

In this section, I start by drawing out some similarities between Levinas and Heidegger concerning what the former calls *ontology* and the latter *metaphysics* in order to approach their take on absolute alterity as a thinking of that which exceeds the classical sense of being as presence.

The question I aim to address is the extent to which David Wood, following Derrida, is right to envisage a thinking of absolute alterity that is more liberal than Levinas's who restricts it to the encounter with the other human being. Responding to Wood's objection to Levinas, I lay out some conditions that an event must meet if it is to be worthy of the name.

* * *

Levinas draws an interesting parallel in *Heidegger, Gagarin, and Us* between modern technology and ethics. They are equally uprooting but in different ways. Modern technology detaches man from his placement in a tradition and native soil, a history and the earth. In a similar vein, ethics suspends man's self-interested behaviour. It overturns his life of enjoyment, labour and possession and produces a different kind of subjectivity. It produces a being that is for-the-other, a generosity and a giving that is without reserve and reservation.

That can happen when the self finds itself exposed to the face of the other. As a figure of weakness and destitution, the face of the other can incite the self to give and take care of him or, conversely, it can incite the self to liquidate the other. The face opens the space of war and peace, of politics and ethics, of the inter-human relation in general.

Levinas suggests at one point that technology might offer an opportunity for an ethical encounter with the other. Once modern technology wrenches us out of 'the Heideggerian world and the superstitions surrounding *Place*', an opportunity appears to us:

> To perceive men outside the situation in which they are placed, and let the human face shine in all its nudity. (Levinas, 1997: 232–3)

Levinas agrees with Heidegger that dwelling or inhabitation is the most profound link that the human being can have to the earth. But he scarcely distinguishes the Heideggerian mode of inhabitation from the reactionary cry for rootedness and the *Blut und Boden* ideology which he obliquely alludes to in the text.

What are we to make of Levinas's reading of Heidegger here and elsewhere and, generally speaking, of the relation between their thinking? That is a question that the argument of the last chapter supposes and that needs to be addressed.

I think that Robert Bernasconi is right when he says that Levinas tends to use Heidegger's ontology as a 'surrogate' for what he (Levinas) wants to oppose to his ethics.[1] In *Heidegger, Gagarin, and Us*, Levinas wants to oppose rootedness in all its forms and variations to the ethical encounter with the face. That encounter effectuates a Copernican turn whereby the other human being, rather than one's native soil and tradition, functions as the zero-point in the orientation to the world.

I do not want to put Levinas on trial for his flawed characterizations of Heidegger's position.[2] Nor do I want to reopen, once more, the debate on whether ontology presupposes ethics, as some Heideggerians and other authors have argued against Levinas. Both have been done before in a more skilful way than I could hope to do. I am thinking of Derrida's (2001a) *Violence and Metaphysics* and, more recently, of François Raffoul's (2005) *Being and the Other: Ethics and Ontology in Levinas and Heidegger*.[3]

What I would like to do instead, in this section, is prepare the ground for a fruitful encounter between Heidegger and Levinas on the thought of absolute difference. To that end, I begin by highlighting a striking proximity between what Levinas calls *ontology* in *Totality and Infinity* and what Heidegger calls *metaphysics* from the 1930s on. With that proximity in mind, it will be easier to identify the reasons why they diverge in their thinking of absolute difference and consider the kind of work to which that notion can be put.

a. Ontology and metaphysics

By *metaphysics*, Heidegger has in mind a forgetting of being or, more precisely, a forgetting of the difference between being and entities. That involves, among other things, an understanding of oneself as a subject for objects in early modernity and, in late modernity, as a resource connected with other resources in the service of industry or a global market.

That forgetting articulates the horizon of the technological age in which any kind of transcendence is nullified, starting with the supersensuous world and the afterlife in distinction from the sensuous world and this mortal life, or the moral law and *the people* as highest values and ends in themselves. That Nietzschean world, which calls for a new interpretation beyond the distinction between the sensuous and the supersensuous (see Chapter 4.5), is understood as a reservoir of energy and forces, as *will to power*. It is seen as 'a global fuel depot or gigantic gas station', in Babette Babich's (2014: 140) apt description.

Being for Heidegger signifies the *way* entities *appear*. It is their 'meaning' or 'ground', which remains essentially inconspicuous or hidden (*BT* 59). Since the Greek beginning in Plato and Aristotle, philosophy has focussed its attention on the kind of entities that appear in the world as well as on the causal laws that unite them in a system rather than on the plurality of modes through which they appear. The difference between being and beings, appearing and the entities that appear, mirrored in language between the verbal and the nominal use of the word *being*, was not thematized. *Being* came to be talked about as a kind of being or causal process.

If what produces a history is not only the act of remembering but, in addition, the forgetting or exclusion that is involved in every act of remembering, then we can say that the forgetting of being constitutes a secret history whose traces can be discerned in the conceptuality of Western thought.

The onto-theological constitution of metaphysics since Aristotle's double or ambiguously formulated project in the *Metaphysics* – the question concerning primary substance, which leads to a theology of immaterial forms and of thought thinking itself, and the question concerning being *qua* being, which, in the course of Western thought, is interpreted as setting out an ontological problematic restricted to an investigation of categories, or the most universal predicates used in propositions – testifies to that forgetting and secret history. The sole thing that deserves attention from Plato and Aristotle onward is *that which* appears and not its *appearance*.

Like metaphysics in Heidegger, what distinguishes *ontology* in Levinas is the primacy of knowledge or, more specifically, the theoretical attitude. It sets the standard of man's relation to beings, including other human beings (Levinas, 1979: 42).

From the primacy of knowledge in Western thought there follows, for Levinas and Heidegger, the primacy of the present as the fundamental mode of time and of presence as the fundamental sense of being. In an interview with Richard Kearney, Levinas says the following:

> According to the Greek model, intelligibility is what can be rendered present, what can be represented in some eternal here and now, exposed and disclosed in pure light. To equate truth thus with presence is to presume that however

different the two terms of a relation might appear (e.g., the Divine and the human) or however separated over time (e.g., into past and future), they can ultimately be rendered commensurate and simultaneous, the same, contained in a history that totalizes time into a beginning or an end, or both, which is presence. The Greek notion of being is essentially this presence. (Kearney, 1986: 19)

Levinas is saying that, in Greek ontology, the present is the index of that which exists and, accordingly, of that which is intelligible, at least according to the Parmenidean identity of thought and being. Only that which exists can be thought, and only that which is present exists (see Aristotle *Physics* IV.10.218a2–3: since the past and the future do not exist, and time is made up of these, it is natural to suppose that time does not exist at all or barely, 'and in the obscure way'). That is why *being* signifies presence. It signifies the intelligibility of entities, which is made possible by the present or by their representation as instances of an unchanging form, species or kind.

Levinas also hears in that classical sense of being *sameness* and *totality*, *coincidence* and *simultaneity*. That which is eminently present is the *nunc stans*, the eternal, which includes these predicates.

In a similar vein, Heidegger contends in his 1927 lecture *The Basic Problems of Phenomenology* that the pre-eminence of the present and its modalities flow from the fact that entities are grasped in the context of the intelligence and sight that governs productive behaviour and activity. An entity properly exists according to Greek metaphysics if it stands on its own or, what amounts to the same thing, if it underlies another but nothing other lies under it. An entity achieves that kind of presence once it has been made or completed, once the course of its production has reached its end. Such an entity is then at hand (*vorhanden*). It is extant (*Anwesen*) in the proper sense. Productive activity has, from the start, had its sight upon the completed and finished work as something self-standing in that sense.

> The verb eina, esse, existere, must be interpreted by way of the meaning of ousia as the present-at-hand and that which is present (*Vorhandenes und Anwesendes*). Being, being-actual, or existing, in the traditional sense, means presence-at-hand. (*BP* 109)[4]

In general, it is always only with reference to worldly entities that being is held in view and that a vocabulary of being is forged. Thus, *being* is conceived as the *essence* or *existence* of entities, as their *underlying substance* or *cause*, as an *a priori condition*, and so on. In such a situation, the alterity of being in relation to entities cannot be recognized.

Ontology for Levinas also involves a reduction of the alterity of the thing aimed at with a theoretical vision to the identity of the concept. The uniqueness of the thing is obliterated once the thing is identified as an instance of a kind and, by implication, as an instance that is replaceable by other instances of the same kind. In that respect, ontology, 'which reduces the other to the same, promotes freedom – the freedom that is the identification of the same, not allowing itself to be alienated by the other' (Levinas, 1979: 42).[5]

b. Absolute alterity

Anything that interrupts intentionality, the correlation of act and object, is situated in a time that exceeds the temporality of consciousness and the privilege it grants to the present as the origin of the intelligibility and manifestation of entities.

That is not to say that this interruption is necessarily *unintelligible* but, rather, that it does not concern the understanding. The affective order – and desire for Levinas (1987a: 62–3), as moods for Heidegger, constitutes that order – gives access to what transcends the present and its modalities. The face of the other indicates a past that was not present to consciousness. The other in his destitution, having always already withdrawn from the light, has always already addressed the self and called for a response and responsibility.

Both Levinas and Heidegger share the same concern. That is to think of a temporality that outstrips the temporality of consciousness and, correlatively, the present and its modalities, and that calls into question presence as the basic meaning of being in Western thought.

I showed in Chapters 1.6 and 2.1 that to think of death as the meaning of the future is to reflect on a difference that does not fall under the categories of being understood as modifications of presence. It is to think, beyond being as presence, of what is absolutely other. That thinking beyond being (*epekeina tês ousias*), to borrow Plato's expression, charts a passage in Heidegger's eyes to another thinking of being (the self-veiling of the clearing). Following Plato more closely than Heidegger, that thinking beyond being and sameness for Levinas makes possible a desire for goodness.

> Goodness consists in taking up a position ... such that the other counts more than myself. (Levinas, 1979: 247)[6]

In Section I of *Totality and Infinity*, Levinas explains that the *I* and the *you* do not form a plurality of I's, that is, a *we* whose members are alike in some respect, alike in gender, race or nationality. The *you* is not other relative to the *I*.

> It is other with an alterity constitutive of the very content of the other. (Levinas, 1979: 39)

L'absolument Autre, c'est Autrui. The other human being is (the) absolutely other.[7] The other is a stranger 'who disturbs the being at home with oneself', the *chez soi* of the *I*.

> But the stranger also means the free one. Over him I have no power. He escapes my grasp by an essential dimension, even if I have him at my disposal. He is not wholly in my site. (Levinas, 1979: 39)

It is as if the stranger approached the *I* as a future that cannot be anticipated, disabling the *I*'s power of self-identification and calling its freedom into question.

Is that statement of identity sound, *the other human being is (the) absolutely other*? In other words, does the meaning of *absolute alterity* exhaust itself in the idea of the other human being? Is David Wood (following Derrida) not right to think of absolute alterity in a less restrictive and more liberal fashion?

> There is a structure to the event, an unexpected transgression of limits that opens unto an unknown future, one that exceeds any attempt to shackle it to the human other. What I am calling for is the event of the event, the explosion of eventuation beyond the boundaries to which Levinas confines it. (Wood, 2005: 67)

Levinas's reason for restricting the idea of absolute alterity to the other human being is not without justification. It seems to be based on his conviction that (a) the face that calls me to respond is the origin of meaning, the source of the phenomenalization of the world, and that (b) what the face is a trace of – the other in his singularity – remains withdrawn or invisible, non-reducible to a context.

(a) Why do I speak to the other? I do not speak to him because I have information or knowledge to give him but, rather, because I have been summoned to respond to what leaves me non-indifferent. That is the weakness or destitution that his face signifies. That signification does not issue from me. It precedes in meaning the totality of possible propositions that we can exchange. The nudity of his face invokes me to respond before anything is said between us. That invocation or *saying* is the origin

of meaning and language. It is the source of the phenomenalization of
the world.

(b) The nudity of his face 'precedes my *Sinngebung* initiative' (Levinas,
     1979: 293). It is the trace of a past that was not present to consciousness.
     The absence it indicates is not modifiable into a presence. It is an absence
     in my world that is originary or non-derivable. The other is, in his
     uniqueness, irreducible to the categories of being as modifications of
     presence.

It follows from both (a) and (b) that the phenomenalization of the world, the
origin of meaning, interrupts the temporality of consciousness and that it
remains irreducible to the meaning of being as presence.

In that respect, it seems that Levinas could not in principle disagree with
Heidegger's claim that the *appearing* of entities, the light that articulates them in
their intelligibility, is not, in turn, an entity. That light has no features by which
it could be described or identified. Being is (the) unidentifiable. Being other
than the totality of entities, it is strangeness pure and simple. In addition, like
the uniqueness of the other human being, it is present in the midst of entities
as an absence or lack that cannot be suppressed or reduced (see Chapters 4.4
and 5.5).

That is also why I am not entirely convinced by Wood's suggestion. I do not
think that any event is as such worthy of the name, certainly not the ground that
it is 'an unexpected transgression of limits that opens unto an unknown future'.
That sounds to me as if any future contingent is an event: whether or not I will
have dinner tomorrow, whether or not there will be a sea-battle tomorrow.

There is a sense in which I think that Wood is right and that his suggestion
can be made to work. An event worthy of the name is an origin of meaning. It is
a source of phenomenalization, like the alterity of death or the singularity of the
other human being. It constitutes an encounter with the absolute limit of thought.
It transpires as a shock or trauma that causes provisional and contingent limits
and restrictions to become unstable or withdraw. But an event that accomplishes
that and is worthy of the name, is, I think, a *figuration of being*. What should be
understood by that expression?

If being (the event of appearing) is distinct from entities, if the distinction
between being and entities is not a distinction between entities, and if, as a result,
to think being is to think of nothing, of nothing determinable or identifiable as
an entity, but also of nothing outside of or beyond entities, then it is perhaps
not possible to think of being in its distinctness from entities except as the

figuration of someone or something, as a figure, precisely, in which the force of the distinction between *someone* and *something*, the *who* and the *what*, has been suspended.

Now that is true of the gods in Heidegger (see Chapter 4.3) and of the guest in his lecture on Hölderlin's *Der Ister* (see Chapter 4.7). It is also true of the feminine in *Totality and Infinity*, which 'is neither a person nor a thing' (Levinas, 1979: 259), and of the *arrivant* in Derrida's *Aporias*.

3. The feminine welcome

I suggested in the last section that an event worthy of the name comes to pass as a figuration of being. My aim in this section is to make that proposition concrete by showing that the feminine in Levinas and the absolute *arrivant* in Derrida, which are two figures of hospitality, are *events* in that sense.

* * *

We have seen that Levinas rejects the Heideggerian mode of inhabitation in *Heidegger, Gagarin, and Us*. That is unfortunate because it forecloses what could have been a productive dialogue with Heidegger's understanding of hospitality in the 1940s.

Dwelling and hospitality are inextricably linked in Heidegger's thought. As I show in Chapter 4.5 and 4.7, Heidegger thinks of a mode of dwelling that can be described as a being for-the-other, as hospitality and generosity towards the unknown and unknowable guest, the divine guest. That mode of dwelling, that hospitality towards the holy, is not an ethics of the other human being. Heidegger conceives it as the fundamental happening of history.

I am not sure that Levinas would refuse to describe that happening as a mode of hospitality. After all, he is clear in *Totality and Infinity* that hospitality and generosity do not always take the form of the ethical encounter with the other human being. Beyond its strictly ethical significance, *hospitality* also signifies the institution of the dwelling by the feminine being.

The dwelling for Levinas is not a possession of the same kind as the goods one collects and keeps at home. That is because the dwelling is constituted by a hospitality. What turns a place or a building into a home or *chez-soi* is an intimacy and familiarity that makes it hospitable to its proprietor. That is what the welcome of the feminine being accomplishes.

[The intimacy of the home] refers us to its essential interiority, and to the inhabitant that inhabits it before every inhabitant, the welcoming one par excellence, the welcome in itself – the feminine being. (Levinas, 1979: 157)

The *feminine* denotes a sexual difference. In Levinas's eyes, the difference between the feminine and the masculine is not a difference of gender or of nature or of kind. He describes sexual difference as an ontological difference in *Ethics and Infinity* and insists that the feminine is not an attribute that applies exclusively to empirical women and the masculine to empirical men. Participation in the feminine and in the masculine is 'the attribute of every human being' (Levinas, 1985: 68).

I am not sure that the feminine is a metaphor, as John Llewelyn (1995: 103) believes, other perhaps than being a metaphor or figuration of being, as I show below. Moreover, Levinas contends in *Time and the Other* that the opposition between the masculine and the feminine does not represent a reciprocity whose terms are equal and complement each other in a whole, as in Aristophanes's account of love in Plato's *Symposium*. The feminine is 'a mode of being that consists in slipping away from the light.... . It is a flight before light' (Levinas, 1987: 87). The feminine is different not relative to the masculine but because alterity constitutes its nature. It is as such that the feminine appears in Levinas's discussion of the dwelling, of the erotic relation, and of fecundity in *Totality and Infinity*.[8]

Levinas might be opposed to an interpretation of the feminine as a figuration of being. The text, however, calls for such an interpretation. Tina Chanter (2003: 51) remarks in *Feminism and the Other* that in 'exploring the withdrawal of the feminine, Levinas claims to improve upon Heidegger's phenomenology of beings'.[9]

There are at least two characteristics of the feminine in Levinas that support such a reading, (a) the equivocal and (b) the hidden.

(a) '[T]he equivocal par excellence' (Levinas, 1979: 255)

Erotic love is equivocal. There is an incontestable element of need and narcissism in it. The beloved understood as an object of need is a middle term in the narcissistic relation of self to self. As Levinas says towards the end of his *Phenomenology of Eros* in *Totality and Infinity*, what the self loves above all else is the love the beloved bears for him (Levinas, 1979: 266). Erotic love aims at the other. But it falls short of her alterity. That is why love dissolves in a relation of immanence, a return to self.

Although erotic love falls short of the other in her alterity, it at times overshoots her alterity and passes beyond her.

> But love also goes beyond the beloved. This is why through the face filters the obscure light coming from beyond the face, from what is not yet, from a future never future enough. (Levinas, 1979: 254)

Love is a need that presupposes the exteriority of the beloved, an exteriority that is manifest in desire. But it goes beyond the beloved as if the beloved had no face, as if she had no ethical transcendence and height, and was unable to command the prohibition of murder.

Levinas (1979: 155) says of the feminine that she is not the formal *you* (*vous*) of the face, but the informal *thou* (*tu*) of familiarity, and that, as 'the source of gentleness in itself', she constitutes the intimacy and familiarity of the home and, by extension, of the gentleness that 'spreads over the face of things' in the world.

That is to say that the feminine is both less and more than the face. *Less* because she makes possible the return to self in love and in the intimacy and recollection of the home. *More* because she makes possible a future that transcends my future death, the child, in fecundity.

That is why the feminine is an event 'situated at the limit of immanence and transcendence' (Levinas, 1979: 254). She articulates the difference between need and desire, ontology and ethics, the return to self and the relation to the other, while being reducible neither to the one nor to the other. As a figure of the limit and transition from the one to the other, she eludes identification.

(b) '[T]he hidden as hidden' (Levinas, 1979: 260)

There is a proximity between Levinas and Nietzsche's thinking of the feminine in this regard. The woman for Nietzsche is also a figure without a determinable identity. Nietzsche writes in his 1886 Preface to *The Gay Science*:

> We no longer believe that truth remains truth when one pulls off the veil; we have lived too much to believe this. Today we consider it a matter of decency not to wish to see everything naked, to be present everywhere, to understand and 'know' everything. 'Is it true that God is everywhere?' a little girl asked her mother; 'I find that indecent!' – a hint for philosophers! One should have more respect for the *bashfulness* with which nature has hidden behind riddles and iridescent uncertainties. Perhaps truth is a woman who has grounds for not showing her grounds? Perhaps her name is – to speak Greek – *Baubo*? (Nietzsche, 2008: 8)

In order to get Demeter to laugh, who was grieving over the abduction of her daughter by Hades, the witch Baubo lifted her skirt and exposed herself.

Nietzsche is not saying that there is a truth to woman that remains veiled in secret, or that nature has veiled her reasons behind appearances. Demeter laughed when Baubo lifted her skirt. Presumably, because she knew that the veil or appearance creates a false depth luring philosophers and men, that it produces the illusion of a hidden, forgotten or disavowed truth, the *maternal phallus*.

What Derrida says of Nietzsche's phrase 'I have forgotten my umbrella' in *Spurs* applies equally well in this instance. That is that its secret is 'the possibility that indeed it might have no secret, that it might only be pretending to be simulating some hidden truth within its folds' (Derrida, 1979: 133).

If the feminine is not a determinable identity, essence or truth, then an entire tradition and philosophical discourse for which correctness and representation, the identity of the subject and of the object constitute privileged and unquestionable values must founder on the thought of the feminine.

Levinas (1987: 85) says in *Time and the Other* that the feminine does not have alterity 'as the reverse side of its identity'. She does not 'comply with the Platonic law of participation where every term contains a sameness and through this sameness contains the Other'. Platonism is overturned in the erotic relation with the feminine being. For this relation describes a situation where difference, far from deriving from the identity of a subject, 'is borne by a being in a positive sense, as essence'. That reversal implies that the secret, understood as the mode of being of the feminine, is not something that depends in its meaning on the prior exposition and revelation of a truth. If there is no truth to the feminine, then the presence of the feminine is the contestation of the primacy of truth over error, of the manifest over the hidden.

No doubt, the 'discretion' (Levinas, 1979: 155) of the feminine presence in Levinas that produces the welcome and intimacy of the home can be read according to the conventional image as the reserved feminine modesty that withdraws to make space for the masculine ego.

That discretion can also signify an absence that is more radical than the absence of the other in the ethical relation. The nudity of the face is the trace of a past that was not present to consciousness. It indicates a being that is altogether other. The feminine signifies a fragility and vulnerability that are without measure. They signify a nudity that is more marked and exposed than the nudity of the face (if such things are comparable). That excessive frailty is feminine tenderness. Its nature is to hide from the light.

If the feminine is the 'hidden, and not a hidden existent' (Levinas, 1979: 264), if it defines the nature or meaning of *concealment* and *secrecy*, then any kind of entity that is hidden participates in the feminine. That is why it must be asked whether the feminine is a figuration of the hiddenness of being. This would imply, conversely, that *being* signifies absolute vulnerability and that sexual difference accomplishes the ontico-ontological difference. Feminine alterity would enact the alterity of being in relation to entities. It would reveal what there is, the world, by founding the home.

That is what Levinas suggests when he presents feminine alterity in *Totality and Infinity* as a modality of being understood in the Heideggerian sense as a modality of disclosure. It establishes the dwelling place as the absolute zero-point in the orientation to the world.

> [T]he dwelling is not situated in the objective world, but the objective world is situated by relation to my dwelling. (Levinas, 1979: 153)

Levinas adds that the feminine welcome that constitutes the intimacy of the home is a presence in discretion. The feminine is revealed 'in its withdrawal and in its absence'. The feminine is something or someone whose 'silent comings and goings' 'reverberate the secret depths of being' (Levinas, 1979: 155–6).

Whatever else Levinas might mean by *the secret depths of being*, it is certainly not reducible to what he thinks under the name of *ontology*. If the feminine is neither a being nor a non-being, if it 'manifests itself at the limit of being and non-being' (Levinas, 1979: 256), then it is right to ask whether the *withdrawal of the feminine* in Levinas can be distinguished from the *withdrawal of being* in Heidegger or, more precisely, whether the former is a rethinking of the latter under the figure – or the non-figure because the non-identity – of the feminine.

4. The absolute *arrivant*

Prior to the ethical hospitality that the host gives the stranger, feminine alterity welcomes the host in his home. A *home* in that sense is not a place with fixed borders and limits and with an identifiable owner. The feminine being that welcomes the host in the intimacy of his house does not own the place, whereas the host finds himself to be as much a guest in his house as the stranger he invites. That is why a *home* is originally a place of exile and refuge (Levinas, 1979: 156).[10] Like Strangers Gate in Central Park, NY, a home originally says

'Welcome! Come on in! Enter freely and without peril!' (Casey, 2011: 42) to both the host and the guest.

But who or what welcomes feminine alterity, 'the welcoming one par excellence, welcome in itself' (Levinas, 1979: 157)? Is it possible to welcome that which makes possible the pre-ethical and the ethical welcome?

There is no welcome of feminine alterity in Levinas. She welcomes and interiorizes, but she is not, in turn, welcomed. At any rate, to welcome feminine alterity is a possibility that, as far as I can see, Levinas does not consider.

Perhaps that is because Levinas restricts hospitality to the other human being whereas the feminine at which the caress aims, being 'neither a person nor a thing' (Levinas, 1979: 259), is not reducible to a member of humanity.

In other words, to welcome the feminine would be to welcome a paradoxical being. On the one hand, she is someone with a 'full human personality' (Levinas, 1979: 155). On the other, she is a being with which I have nothing in common, seeing as she is neither a *who* nor a *what*. Ambiguous in the extreme, she has no determinable identity. She is a being, if she exists, whose content is determined by alterity and strangeness pure and simple.[11]

To welcome the feminine being is like welcoming the absolute *arrivant*. Like feminine alterity, Derrida says of the absolute *arrivant* that it 'does not yet have a name or identity' (Derrida, 1993: 34). What interests Derrida in the French word *arrivant* is that its meaning is neutral between something and someone that arrives, the *who* and the *what*.

> The new *arrivant*, this word can, indeed, mean the neutrality of *that which* arrives, but also the singularity of *who* arrives. (Derrida, 1993: 33)

The absolute *arrivant* is, like the feminine, without any identifiable characteristic. It is an absolute stranger or strangeness itself.

What I take Derrida to be doing (among other things) in *Aporias* where he proceeds to determine the absolute *arrivant* by negation – it is *not* what crosses a threshold between two identifiable places, it is *not* an occupier, *not* a refugee, *not* this, *not* that, etc. (see Derrida, 1993: 34) – is to invite us to engage in a thinking that takes place at the limit of the ontic (thing, person) and the ontological (event of appearing). The absolute *arrivant* is a figuration of being.

> [T]he absolute *arrivant* makes possible everything to which I have just said it cannot be reduced, starting with the humanity of man. (Derrida, 1993: 35)

The other thing that I take Derrida to be doing with the (non-) figure of the absolute *arrivant* is to attempt to think a relation of hospitality that is not restricted by any conditions, that is not bound by any expectations, that does not limit itself to a specific other, say, to a friend rather than to an enemy, to a human being rather than to an animal, to a living thing rather than to a non-living thing.

This relation of hospitality that is open to the human and to the non-human alike is a relation with a future that is more radically other than the ethical relation with the other human being in Levinas. It is a future that is without precedent in the past or present; it is singular in the extreme. That hospitality towards the future, as we shall see in Chapter 4.5, is also how Heidegger thinks of the relation with the earth in his first lecture on Hölderlin.

The absolute *arrivant* is the correlate of unconditional hospitality, which Derrida distinguishes from conditional hospitality. Conditional hospitality is hospitality given to a stranger on the basis of conditions such that the host keeps his authority as host and master of the house, 'and thereby affirms the law of hospitality as the law of his household'. This condition involves the principle of identity, the self-identity of the host, 'the *being oneself at home with oneself*. I cannot offer you hospitality without saying, 'that is mine, I am at home' (Derrida, 2000: 4; 14).

Unconditional hospitality, by contrast, transcends the laws of hospitality. It is an intentional experience that carries itself, beyond knowing, 'toward the other as absolute stranger, as unknown, where I know that I know nothing of him', whether he is a friend or enemy, an animal, human or god or whether he is the Messiah (Derrida, 2000: 8).

As Derrida puts it elsewhere, unlike sending someone an invitation, where I expect and am prepared to receive the other, where there is no surprise, a visitation implies the arrival of someone who is not expected, 'who can show up at any time'. Unconditional hospitality is a relation with the future in its imminence. To be unconditionally hospitable is to welcome the visitation rather than the invited guest.

> I must be unprepared, or prepared to be unprepared, for the unexpected arrival
> of *any* other. (Derrida, 1999: 70)

That experience, which unsettles the identity of the host *qua* host, as if he suffered a symbolic death and became the guest received in his own home by the other, is the impossible event of justice.

* * *

I have shown in this chapter that what makes an event worthy of the name is its behaviour as a figuration of being. An event is a figuration of being if it is without a determinable identity (and, thus, produces a shock) and if it is an origin of meaning. I analysed briefly the figure of the feminine in Levinas and of the absolute *arrivant* in Derrida to show that they can be seen as events in that sense. In the next chapter, I show that the same is true of Heidegger's gods and of the guest in his lectures on Hölderlin.

4

Dwelling

Die Zeit der Gott-losigkeit enthält das Unentschiedene des erst Sichentscheidenden.

—Martin Heidegger, *'Andenken'*

'You'll learn that in this house it's hard to be a stranger. You'll also learn that it's not easy to stop being one.'

—Maurice Blanchot, *The Idyll*

1. Introduction

According to Heidegger's thought in the 1930s and 1940s, dwelling involves a tensed relation between the unhomely and the homely. The *unhomely* denotes a future that is without common measure with the present. It is identical neither with one's death (Chapter 1) nor with the other human being (Chapter 2) but, rather, with being. In this chapter, I show that the gods, the earth and the foreign guest are, in Heidegger's text, figurations of being in that sense (see Chapter 3). I show that to dwell is to relate to the unhomely as the basis and ground of the homely.

Accordingly, *dwelling* is a notion that thinks the relation between the human Dasein and being. That relation constitutes a community whose members are entirely dissimilar. Being is other than the totality of entities, including the human Dasein. It is the light that articulates entities in their intelligibility and that is not itself, in turn, an entity. Is a community of absolute dissimilars possible, a community of those who have nothing in common, to borrow the title of Alphonso Lingis's (1994) book? That is the question I aim to address in this chapter.

Dwelling does not describe a community between two strangers who are members of humanity, as in Levinas or Lingis. It is a community between the human being and what is other than human, indeed, other than the totality of entities, a *stranger* in a more fundamental sense of the term than in Levinas or Lingis.

As I intend to demonstrate in the course of this chapter, Heidegger presents at least two ways in which such a community can come to pass and one way in which it comes to ruin. It comes to pass in holy mourning (section 5) and guestfriendship (section 7), and it comes to ruin in the figure of Antigone (section 4).

I begin in section 2 by explaining the different senses in which the earth can be considered the unhomely basis of the homely in Heidegger. In section 3, I clarify the senses in which the theme of the retreat of the gods can be read.

Section 4 teases out a paradox in Heidegger's reading of *Antigone* in his 1942 *Der Ister* lecture. The lesson he appears to draw from the text is that to belong to being and death in an authentic way brings about the ruin of the human Dasein, in other words, that authenticity is impossible.

In section 5, I show that that is otherwise with regard to the relation between the human Dasein and the gods. Holy mourning makes possible a community of absolute dissimilars.

In section 6, I explain how a thinking of hospitality arises in Heidegger. In section 7, I explain his notion of hospitality, the greeting and the guest. I argue that like holy mourning, guestfriendship constitutes a community with being that does not bring about the collapse of the human Dasein.

2. The earth

In this section, I lay out the various senses in which the earth can be considered the unhomely basis of the homely by drawing on parts of Heidegger's reading of Hölderlin's *Der Ister* and *Germania*. I return to some of these senses in section 4 where I discuss *Antigone* and show in what way Antigone's belonging to death and the law of the earth leads to her ruin.

I return to the notion of the earth in section 5 as well, where I show how the poet relates to it in holy mourning. Far from bringing about his ruin, the earth appears as the futural horizon on which the poet projects a homeland.

* * *

Hölderlin writes in the first and final stanzas of *Der Ister*:

> For rivers make arable
> The land

. . .

The rock, however, has need of cuts

And of furrows the earth,

Inhospitable it would be, without while. (Cited in *HH* 5–6)

The images of *the river* and of *the while* operate on two levels in Heidegger/Hölderlin.[1] They describe the mode of being of the poet as a figure that establishes a discursive relation between the human being and the gods and, as such, a figure that makes possible a historical community. They also describe the dwelling place of the human being. In what follows, I focus on the latter sense of the images in Heidegger's lecture on *Der Ister*.

The river is an image of the essence of place. Heidegger describes it in the lecture as the locality of the locale (*Ortschaft des Ort*). It is also an image of the essence of time, which he describes as an event of migration, wandering or journeying (*Wanderschaft*) (*HH* 30).

To paraphrase what Heidegger says of technology, the *essence* of place is not itself a place, a geographical location. It is not a region on planet earth, a territory, a settlement or a point in Euclidean space. Doubtless, it denotes the dwelling place of man. But it is not as if that dwelling is identifiable in a specific location in distinction from another, as if dwelling takes place *here* instead of *there*. No, the dwelling denotes an absolute *here*, a zero-point that orients the world and gives it structure and meaning.

More precisely, *to dwell* does not mean, in the first instance, to reside somewhere. As Heidegger uses the word, it means to become at home on the earth. In this becoming-at-home, the human being fulfils its historical vocation. That is why the *essence* of place is best understood, not as a place, but as a *becoming*, a journey or migration from the foreign to the proper, as I show in sections 6 and 7.

> The river '*is*' the locality that pervades the abode of human beings upon the earth, determines them to where they belong and where they are homely (*heimisch*). The river thus brings human beings into what is proper to them (*das Eigene*) and maintains them in what is their own. Whatever is proper to them is that to which human beings belong and must belong if they are to fulfil whatever is destined to them, and whatever is fitting (*Schickliche*), as their specific way of being. (*HH* 21)

What is the historical vocation of the human being? What is proper to him? It is to win 'the earth as the "ground" of the homely (*"Grund" des Heimischen*)' (*HH* 30). Heidegger says something similar in *The Origin of the Work of Art*. He writes that upon 'the earth and in it, historical man grounds his dwelling in the world' (*PLT* 46).

What does *the earth* mean here? In what respect is it *the ground* or *basis* of what is homely? Isn't the earth something uncanny, foreign and difficult to understand?

The dead are laid to rest in it. Or their ashes are scattered over it. As the final resting place, we relate to the earth as a site of mourning. *The earth* does not here mean a planet in the solar system. Before being conceived as such, it is experienced as a holy sanctum. It is a place of refuge for the dead that remains cloaked in 'eternal darkness', as Antigone describes it in *Oedipus at Colonus* (Sophocles, 2009: 132).

Derrida remarks in *Of Hospitality* that the final resting place situates the *ethos*, 'the key habitation for defining home, the city or country where relatives, father, mother, grandparents are at rest'.

> [I]t is the place of immobility from which to measure all the journeys and all the distancings. (Derrida, 2000a: 87)

The earth as final resting place constitutes an absolute *here*, a zero-point in the orientation to the world, tradition and history.

In accordance with Antigone's description of the earth in *Oedipus at Colonus*, Heidegger thinks it as 'essentially self-secluding' (*PLT* 47) in *The Origin of the Work of Art*. He means by that at least three things:

(a) The qualitative experience of nature resists quantification, measure or, generally speaking, the understanding. The earth, as Heidegger puts it, is a place of unmeasure (*Unmass*) or excess (*PLT* 70).

   What is true of the stone in my hand, for instance, is not true of its objective weight. The stone in my hand is heavy. But a stone that weighs 3 kg is *in itself* not heavier than a stone that weighs 5 kg. *Heaviness* is, in Locke's phrase, a secondary quality. It is not an intrinsic quality of the stone. It applies relative to a being whose experience of the world is mediated by its embodiment. The terms we use to describe the stone's heaviness cannot be translated in the terms we use to describe its weight.

   Again, the colour of the sky shines brightly on sunny days. But the wavelengths of which the blue of the sky consists do not shine. The terms we use to describe the shining quality of the sky cannot be translated in the terms we use to describe its wavelengths. 'Earth thus shatters every attempt to penetrate into it' (*PLT* 47).

(b) The authentic relation to the earth is affective. Its resistance to the understanding is felt before being understood. Heidegger speaks of the earth at one point as a 'silent call' in his description of Van Gogh's painting of a pair of peasant shoes (*PLT* 34). That is to say that the earth affectively disposes the peasant woman to her world.

(c) The earth is the origin of the clearing. The clearing originates, or expressly comes to light, in an experience of the limit of the understanding (which is coextensive with the limit of history or the world). When language and meaning fail in anxiety, entities press upon the human Dasein in their entirety in their undifferentiated presence. That presence of the whole is the clearing. Heidegger writes:

> Beings refuse themselves to us down to that one and seemingly least feature which we touch upon most readily when we can say no more of beings than that they are. Concealment as refusal is not simply and only the limit of knowledge in any given circumstance, but the beginning of the clearing of what is lighted. (*PLT* 53–4)

Like death, the earth constitutes the limit of what can be understood. It is the basis on which a historical world has always already been projected. More ancient than history, meaning and the idiomatic languages of historical peoples, the earth is a thrown basis that cannot be retrieved in a project. It is manifest in moods, or in the way it attunes a people to its world, as an origin in retreat.

Or what amounts to the same thing from a different angle, the earth denotes that which lies ahead of every project. It is there, like death, as the non-contingent limit and horizon of the possible. It is on the basis of the earth as futural horizon, as I show in section 5, that the decisions and differentiations that found a world are articulated.

One of these decisions concerns the relation between the human being and the gods. In the lecture on *Germania*, Heidegger writes that the earth is the place where gods are nurtured.

> The earth is here experienced in advance in the lucidity of a questioning knowing concerning the historical mission of a people (*geschichtliche Sendung eines Volkes*). The native earth (*heimatliche Erde*) here is not a mere space delimited by external borders, a realm of nature, or a locality constituting a possible venue for this or that event to be played out. *Die Erde als diese heimatliche für die Götter erzogen*. This singular native earth is nurtured for the gods. It first becomes a home (*Heimat*) through such cultivation, but it can also as such decline and fall

back into a mere place of residence (*Wohnsitz*), which accordingly goes hand in
hand with godlessness. (*HGR* 95)

What is it to nurture the earth for the gods? I doubt it means to build churches
or temples.

There are at least two ways of making sense of this. The first is Heidegger's
discussion of *daimonia* and the gods in his *Parmenides* lecture. The second is his
discussion of the passing away of the last god and of the retreat of the gods in
Contributions to Philosophy: From the Event.

The *Parmenides* lecture (1942–3) was delivered approximately seven
years after this passage from the lecture on *Germania* (1934–5) was written.
Nevertheless, this later lecture seems to reflect a developing train of thought
concerning the link between the earth, the gods and the human being that can
be traced from this lecture on *Germania* to the *Parmenides* lecture, passing
through the *Contributions to Philosophy: From the Event* (*CP*, 1936–8).

3. The gods

I showed in the last section that the earth is the limit of the understanding. In
the next section on *Antigone*, I consider to what extent it is possible to belong
to the earth.

In this section, I turn to the *Parmenides* lecture and the *Contributions to
Philosophy: From the Event* to shed some light on the connection between the
earth and the gods that Heidegger first highlights in his *Germania* lecture.
I argue in this section that the gods are, like the earth, figurations of being and
time. This means that they are historico-ontological conditions of possibility of
the authentic historical existence of a people.

In section 5, I return to this discussion of the gods and the earth to show that,
in holy mourning, the poet relates to them as the horizon on which he projects
a homeland.

* * *

Like the feminine in Levinas and the absolute *arrivant* in Derrida (see Chapter 3.3
and 3.4), the gods in Heidegger are figurations of being.

The divine in the Greek sense, *to theion*, is precisely being itself looking into the
ordinary. (*P* 115)

The role played by the gods in Heidegger's work in the 1930s and 1940s is
reminiscent of the role played by the voice of conscience in *Being and Time* (see
Chapter 2.4).

Heidegger describes the mode of being of the gods by reference to the look and saying (*das Blicken und das Sagen*). *Saying* does not mean vocal utterance. The gods have no vocal organs. They speak by staying silent. It is a silence that gives something to be understood through a mood such as respect, grace, awe or mourning. The gods are the attuning ones (*die Stimmenden*) (P 111).

No doubt, *to look* does also not mean in this instance what we ordinarily take it to mean, that is, to make something transparent, to cast light on it or to make it present as an object for a subject.

Heidegger tells us that, for Greek thought, the emphasis is on the one who looks rather than on the thing that is being looked at. In looking, the one who looks comes into view. The look is experienced as that in which the other who looks appears and stands in view, as that in which the self awaits the other who looks (*entgegenwartende Blicken*) (P 103).

The one who looks in a pre-eminent sense is not the human being. It is the gods. The human being is first experienced as a being that is 'looked upon' (P 108) by the other.[2]

As figurations of being, the gods look into the ordinary and come into view as remarkable beings. Heidegger uses *Ungeheure* (P 104) for my bland *remarkable*. The gods that come into view are uncanny, monstrous, strange or excessive. That seems to mean at least two things:

- By looking into the ordinary world, and by thus coming into view before the human being, the gods make themselves and the world conspicuous.

  The Greek *daimonia*, which Heidegger translates as *Ungeheure*, signifies both the uncanny and the divine. The uncanny is not the exception to the rule. It is the revelation of the ordinary. That is what the gods accomplish.
- The gods are not, strictly speaking, identifiable with worldly beings or, what amounts to the same thing, with agencies of a certain kind.

Heidegger is clear, particularly in *Contributions to Philosophy: From the Event*, that if we are to think of the gods properly, then we must think of them beyond the constraints of ontotheology. That means (among other things) that the gods cannot be thought of as either natural or supernatural causes or as the kind of entities to which existence can apply as a predicate, as in the debate between the theist and the atheist where the first affirms, and the second denies, that *existence* applies to God.

> To speak of 'the gods' does of course not mean that a decision has been made here affirming the existence of many gods instead of one; rather, it is meant to indicate the undecidability of the being of the gods, whether one or many. This

undecidability carries within it the question of whether something like being can be attributed to gods at all without destroying everything divine. To speak of 'the gods' is to name the undecidability as to whether a god, and which god, could arise once again as an extreme distress for which essence of the human being in which way. (*CP* 345)

Heidegger thinks of the gods neither as charismatic figures that ground community life, as Julian Young (2002: 35) believes, nor as objects of worship, as Benjamin Crowe (2007: 238) insists. As I see it, they are figurations of time – not of chronological time understood as a succession of nows but, rather, of historical time.

The absence that defines the historical future (not-yet) is not a modality of the present. It is not a future that will sooner or later become present. Heidegger describes this future in *Contributions to Philosophy: From the Event* by reference to the passing away of the last god. Levinas thinks of the relation with the other human being as a relation with the future. In a similar vein, Heidegger thinks of the relation with the last god as a relation with the historical future.

Let me highlight two things about the passing away of the last god:

(a) In the first place, the passing away of the last god is a possibility that articulates, and that opens the human being to, the absolute impossibility of any historical world. It is the counterpart, at the level of historical thinking, of being-toward-death in the existential analytic. In his explanation of the meaning of *last* in the expression *the last god*, Heidegger writes that it does not mean *stopping* or *cessation* but *origin* or *beginning*. He then adds,

> If we have such a poor grasp of "death" in its extremity (*in seinem Äußersten*), then how will we ever measure up to the rare beckoning of the last god? (*CP* 321)

If *death* signifies the absolute limit of existence, then *the last god* must signify the absolute limit of history. But we think of death poorly when we think of it as the cessation of life. So presumably we think of the last god poorly when we think of it as the cessation of history understood as a chronological sequence of events.

Death, the absolute limit of my existence, makes it conspicuous as irreplaceably mine and as something for which I must take responsibility. In that sense, death is a beginning or origin. Presumably, the poet's encounter with the last god would make conspicuous the history into which a particular humanity had been thrown as its own and as something for which it must take responsibility.

Heidegger describes that encounter as a beckoning. To beckon is to a give a sign to the other. On leaving, for example, I wave my hand in the air to say goodbye to my friend. That sign tokens the proximity that endures between us even as 'the distance increases'. Conversely, my friend arrives and waves his hand at me. That tokens 'the distance that still prevails in this felicitous proximity' (*HGR* 31).

The relation between the human being and the gods is envisaged in that way too. It is a relation of distance in proximity and of proximity in distance. That relation is accomplished by the poet as remembrance and awaiting. It is the antithesis of the mystical unification of man with the gods (or Nature) yearned for by some of the early Romantics.

(b) What is meant by *passing away* in the expression *the passing away of the last god*? In one sense, that phrase suggests that the last god is not something that can be made intelligible in terms of the present and its modalities. The last god is not a worldly entity that could one day arrive like the Messiah or that was once present in some bygone time.

Heidegger cites a sentence from one of Hölderlin's fragments in his *Germania* lecture. The sentence reads, 'Thus everything heavenly passes quickly.' He then comments:

> To pass does not here mean to perish, but rather to pass away, not to remain, not to remain there as something that is constantly present, i.e., thought in terms of the matter, to appear as something that has been (*Gewesendes*), to appear in a coming that presses upon us (*einem kommenden Andrang*). (*HGR* 101)

Like death, the last god is not present in the mode of the present. It is there as either not yet or no longer there. Or better yet, the last god is nothing save the ecstatic movement of historical time. It is the constant return and projection of that which has been *as* what is to come at any moment.

Put differently, the phrase *passing away* thinks the gods as figures of absence. That does not mean that the *retreat of the gods* is a metaphor that refers to a certain number of historical events in the past, such as the demise of the Greek or Roman age, the death of Christ on the cross or the secularism of the modern age. Instead, the absence of the gods is a possibility that can come to light at any moment. It is an absence that hesitates between arrival and flight (*Ankunft und Flucht*), approach and withdrawal (*Anfall und Ausbleib*).

Once the modern age is understood by the poet as the age of the retreat of the gods, and this *retreat* is understood in its ambiguity as signifying their imminent arrival *or* irreversible withdrawal, a particular humanity faces a crisis with respect to its way of being. Can it continue to live in forgetfulness of their absence? Or can it start living in remembrance of their departure and await their imminent return?

To experience the retreat of the gods in this way is, I think, one of the historico-ontological conditions of possibility for a particular humanity to enter a time of decision. It makes possible a transition to another beginning of history.

* * *

I started this discussion on the gods after citing a passage from Heidegger's *Germania* lecture in the last section. The passage says that the native earth is nurtured for the gods. Given what I have shown in this section, I think that we can safely assume what that passage means. Exposing himself to and poetizing the retreat of the gods – that is, their imminent arrival *or* irreversible flight – the poet articulates the undecidability that constitutes the historical future.

At bottom, I think, the earth is this abyssal future from which there originates a destiny or history for a people or, more precisely, in the horizon of which a people can draw a homeland for the first time.

> The great, pivotal times of the peoples (*Wendezeiten der Völker*) always emerge from the abyss, and, in each case, in accordance with the extent to which a people reaches into it – which is to say, into its earth – and possess homeland (*Heimat besitzt*).[3]

Heidegger adds that the gods are 'earthly'. He explains:

> 'Earthly' does not mean created by a creator-god, but rather an uncreated abyss within which all emergent happening (*heraufkommende Geschehen*) trembles and remains preserved. (*HGR* 97)

In section 5, I show that what makes the Hesperian poet unique is the fact that his poetry enacts the retreat of the gods. It remembers their flight and awaits their imminent return in holy mourning.

4. *Antigone*

I showed in the last section that, for Heidegger, a people posits a home in the horizon of its native earth. My aim in this section is to show that, by his 1942 *Der Ister* lecture, he seems to have acquired a more tragic and pessimistic outlook on the matter. In a sense, his reading of *Antigone* suggests that an authentic community between the human Dasein and the earth (being) is impossible.

* * *

The drama of *Antigone* begins the day after the end of the civil war between Eteocles and Polyneices. Polyneices has led a foreign force to attack Thebes. The attackers were defeated and, in the fray, the brothers Eteocles and Polyneices killed each other.

Creon, the ruler of Thebes, decrees that no fallen enemy of the city shall be mourned and given the customary burial rites. It is Antigone's duty, however, as Polyneices and Eteocles's sister, to look after their burial and perform the proper rites. She tells her sister, Ismene:

> Creon ordains – the thought drives me mad! –
> honor for one, dishonour for the other.
> Eteocles, so they say, he has treated with justice and customary law,
> laid him in earth, to be honored by the dead below.
> As for the battered corpse of Polyneices –
> they say it is proclaimed to all the city –
> no one is allowed to mourn or entomb,
> but must leave it unburied and unwept, like carrion,
> sweet pickings for the birds' pleasure. (Sophocles, 2009: 140)

She defies Creon's rule and buries Polyneices. Her punishment is to be entombed alive.

When Creon tells her, towards the end of the drama, that she knowingly defied his rule, she justifies her action by appealing to a different kind of law than divine justice and the laws that mortals decree for themselves to live together in cities.

> Zeus did not command these things,
> nor did Justice, who dwells with the gods below,
> ordain such laws for men.
> Neither do I believe that your decrees,
> or those of any other mortal, are strong enough to overrule
> the ancient, unwritten, immutable laws of the gods,
> which are not for the present alone, but have always
> been – and no one knows when they began. (Sophocles, 2009: 155)

The tragic conflict between Antigone and Creon is not the conflict between the divine and human law, as Hegel (1977: 266) insists. Antigone says that the law that governs her action transcends the upper and lower gods, Zeus and Justice. In one respect, her law issues from beyond the divine sphere. In another, however, it is part of the 'unwritten, immutable laws of the gods'.

Moreover, Creon decrees his law before the gods (Sophocles, 2009: 149). That makes it a part of the divine sphere. But that does not exclude that it is also part of the human sphere.

Oudemans and Lardinois's (1987: 129) interpretation of *Antigone* in *Tragic Ambiguity* is close to Heidegger's reading of the text in his *Der Ister* lecture. Like Heidegger, they claim that the whole drama is concentrated in the little word *deinos* that appears several times in *Antigone* and, most importantly, in the first stasimon, the choral Ode to Man. It is, they say, 'the key word of the tragedy'.

The chorus in the first stasimon refers to man's daring (*tolma*). That daring is ambiguous in the extreme. The human being subdues the forces of nature and establishes order thanks to his passion (*orge*), cunning and skill. But the same passion also drives him to transgress limits, to confuse justice with injustice and to commit *hubris*. That is what is terrible and awe-inspiring (*deinos*) about the human being. The passion that drives him to found civilization changes into wrath, and causes civilization to founder. According to Oudemans and Lardinois (1987: 129–30), the tragic structure that constitutes the human being as *to deinon* is such that he will never be able to harmonize order and excessive power.

Heidegger agrees that the daring that the chorus refers to in the Ode to Man is ambiguous. But that daring is not the passion that drives the human being to establish order and transgress limits. It is a daring or risk that consists in having to choose and distinguish between two ways of being, two antithetical modalities of the essence of the human being defined as *deinon*.

> [T]he risk of distinguishing and deciding between that being unhomely proper to the human being and a being unhomely that is inappropriate. Antigone herself is this supreme risk [or daring, *tolma*] within the realm of the *deinon*. To be this risk is her essence. (*HH* 117)

The tragic conflict for Heidegger is between two ways of being unhomely, remembrance and forgetfulness of the hearth, belonging and not belonging to being, represented by Antigone and Creon respectively.

Heidegger justifies his interpretation by connecting the first two sentences of the choral ode that describe the essence of the human being as *to deinon* with the final three lines. His translation of the beginning of the choral ode reads:

> Manifold is the uncanny (*das Unheimliche, ta deina*), yet nothing
> more uncanny looms or stirs beyond the human being.

His translation of the final three lines reads:

> Such shall not be entrusted to my hearth (*Herde, estios*)
> nor share their delusion with my knowing,
> who put such a thing to work. (*HH* 60–1)

Heidegger makes explicit the connection between the first and final sentences by translating *to deinon* as *das Unheimliche, the uncanny*, and by interpreting the latter as *das Unheimische, the unhomely*. That interpretation brings into play the contrast and tension with the hearth and home that the chorus refers to in the final three sentences. That is the tension that Heidegger sees in the drama – the tension, namely, between being unhomely and being homely.

In the first lines of the ode, the chorus is not merely making a comparative statement to the effect that some things are more uncanny than others and that the human being is highest in the order of uncanny things, as if uncanniness was an extrinsic quality of the human being. The chorus thinks of the human being as a being that is in its essence uncanny. It is on that basis that it can speak comparatively of things, including of the power of nature, as being more or less uncanny than other things.

In the final lines of the ode, the chorus excludes someone from the hearth or home. The chorus prays that it will not have to share its knowledge with the delusion of this unhomely being. Who is the chorus excluding from the home? Who is the unhomely one?

The chorus excludes from the hearth those who, having acted rashly, are without city. Those who upset the order of the city are also barred from the domestic hearth. It is clearly not the human being spoken of in the first lines – that is, the human being defined in its essence as the unhomely one – who is excluded. The chorus rejects a particular way of being unhomely. It excludes those who are forgetful of the hearth, notably Creon.

Oudemans and Lardinois's (1987: 127) interpretation of the oxymoron *upsipolis apolis* in the choral ode supports this reading. They contend that this phrase suggests that the ruler and the outcast, the person who is high in the city (*upsipolis*) and the person who is without city (*apolis*) might exchange places or even become one and the same.[4]

Those whom the chorus excludes from the hearth are those who live in forgetfulness of being, inasmuch as being is the hearth, *Das Sein ist der Herd* (*HH* 112). Heidegger's interpretation of the hearth as being does not seem to me to be entirely outlandish, as Dennis Schmidt (2001: 259) claims in *On Germans and Other Greeks: Tragedy and Ethical Life* when he remarks that Heidegger 'ontologizes beyond the limits of ontology'.

True, the chorus and the characters nowhere speak of being in *Antigone*. However, the law to which Antigone appeals to justify her action in defiance of Creon's decree is the law of the hearth and that law transcends in some respect both the divine and human spheres. It is a sacred law that prevails always. Its origin is unknown. No amount of human cunning and intelligence can defeat it. It is, like death, the impossible, that against which nothing can avail (*tamechana*) (Sophocles, 2009: 90).

The law of the hearth is the law of being insofar as it does not derive from entities. In particular, it is not reducible to the laws of kinship and blood relation.

> We must think beyond the cult of the dead and blood-relatedness and retain the word of Antigone as it is said. We can then recognize that, thought in a Greek sense, she names being itself. This is the ground of being homely, the hearth. (*HH* 118)

Since the law that Antigone cites in defence of her action is not relative to and does not vary with historical worlds, we can say that it is a law of the earth, of what is trans-historical and self-secluding.

Heidegger cites the Pythagorean thinker Philolaos in support of his interpretation. Philolaos describes the hearth as the one (*to en*) that unifies what there is. He then contextualizes Philaloas's talk within the pre-Socratic thinking of *phusis*.

> For the essence of being for the Greeks is *phusis* – that illumination that emerges of its own accord and is mediated by nothing else, but is itself the middle. (*HH* 112)

Heidegger does not dispute that the Greek for *hearth* typically refers to the goddess *Estia* that presides at the centre of the household and at the communal hearth of the city. He wants to say that, in addition to referring to entities in the world, the word invariably signifies being.

In that sense, the hearth is the light that permeates entities in their entirety. It illuminates them through a play of contrast and difference. Entities detach themselves from the background with which they were initially fused and come to stand in relief against each other. *Being* is that light that makes entities intelligible through this movement of differentiation (*Aus-einander-setzung*) (see *EHP* 76).[5]

That light is, however, difficult to grasp, because it has no outline or shape by which it could be described, let alone identified, against a backdrop. Exposure to that light, if that were possible, would be exposure to nothingness, loss of orientation, loss of self, anxiety. That is why that light hides itself in beings, namely, so that the human Dasein can engage with others in discourse and talk about things. The ground of the intelligibility of entities, or of a particular historical world, is a light that veils itself in the midst of entities. That self-veiling light is the earth.

That is what makes Antigone supremely uncanny. She chooses to belong to what is other than entities at the cost of her life.

Perhaps that is the sense of the tragic that Heidegger intends to convey in his *Der Ister* lecture. There is no belonging to being that does not, at the same time, bring the human being to ruin, insofar as such belonging takes place in a transgression and exceeding of limits. To transgress entities in the direction of their being is to risk losing one's self. It is to explicitly open oneself to nothingness and death.

5. Holy mourning

In the last section, I showed that Heidegger seems to suggest in his *Der Ister* lecture that to belong to the earth does not happen without bringing about the collapse of the human Dasein.

In this section, I return to the conclusion I arrived at in section 3 with regard to the retreat of the gods and argue that holy mourning presents a way of belonging that does not lead to the ruin of the human Dasein.

* * *

Heidegger compares holy mourning with mourning one's beloved in his *Germania* lecture.

> No longer being allowed to call upon the gods (*Götter*) of old, this will to acquiesce in abandonment, what else is it? – it is nothing else than the sole possible, resolute readiness for awaiting the divine (*Göttlichen*); for the gods as such can be relinquished in such abandonment only if they are retained in their divinity … Where the most beloved (*das Liebste*) has left, love (*die Liebe*) remains behind, for otherwise the former could not have left at all. (*HGR* 85–6)

The argument turns on the difference between what the concrete and the abstract noun signify, *das Liebste* and *die Liebe*, *der Götter* and *das Göttlichen*. The abstract noun – *love* and *the divine* – does not designate an abstract entity, a universal.

What remains when my beloved has abandoned me? To properly mourn her consists of renouncing her and in letting her go. What remains when I am so constrained to let her go? Nothing save love as an unfilled and empty possibility.

Mourning my beloved, I find myself face-to-face with love as a failed possibility. I find myself awaiting its fulfilment.

To be sure, in a sense, I await the impossible. My beloved is irrevocably gone, and there is no other who could conceivably replace her. To mourn my beloved is, in a sense, to endure and suffer the impossible fulfilment of love.

I don't think that holy mourning is different from mourning one's beloved. To mourn the absence of the gods is to renounce them and let them go. It is to stand face-to-face with the divine as an unfilled and empty possibility. It is to suffer its impossible fulfilment. 'Holy names are lacking', Hölderlin writes in *Homecoming*. 'That the gods have fled does not mean that divinity (*Göttlichkeit*) too has vanished from the Dasein of human beings. Here it means that such divinity precisely prevails, yet as something no longer fulfilled, as becoming dark and overcast, yet still powerful' (*HGR* 86). The divine as an unfilled historical possibility makes conspicuous the absence of the gods. As I remarked in section 3, that absence is intrinsically ambiguous. It can signify their imminent arrival *or* irreversible withdrawal. In neither of these cases, however, should we think that what is at stake is a modality of the present, as if the gods will one day be present to man as worldly beings or as if they were once present to him as such in the past.

Heidegger remarks that holy mourning does not only mean that the poet, in his poetry, renounces the gods that have flown, it also means that the poet unconditionally awaits (*unbedingte Erharren*) their return and imminent arrival (*HGR* 106). What I take Heidegger to be saying is something similar to what Derrida has in mind with the unconditional hospitality of the absolute *arrivant* (see Chapter 3.4).

The awaiting that Heidegger speaks of is not conditioned in its content by the gods or God that human beings have worshipped in the past or that they claim for themselves in the present. To await the return of the gods is not to await some entity in the world. It is to accomplish a relation with the earth as the horizon in which a homeland or world is posited for the first time.

Why is the earth that horizon? The earth is the ground on which a particular historical humanity has always already been thrown. It can always return, therefore, in the projection of the poet, as a possibility against which that humanity can draw a home for itself.

Like death, however, the earth is not a possibility like some other. It is singular and self-secluding. It is already there or yet to come. It eludes identification and the present. The earth is the temporality of being as history or destiny.

6. The proper and the foreign

I showed in section 2 that the image of *the river* in the *Der Ister* lecture describes a journey from the foreign to the proper, a *becoming at home* on the earth. What was said in the last section about holy mourning, that it consists of projecting the earth as the horizon from which a homeland can be drawn for a people, is one way of cashing out that *becoming at home* on the earth.

In the next section, I argue that guestfriendship is another way of cashing out that becoming at home. In this section, I explain how a thinking of hospitality arises in Heidegger and what distinguishes his reading of the relation between the foreign and the proper in Hölderlin's letter to Böhlendorff from the usual reading.

* * *

Heidegger deepens his notion of becoming at home in the undelivered Part III of the *Der Ister* lecture. It recalls some of the motifs of his lecture on Hölderlin's *Andenken* of the previous year in 1941/2.

That is no accident. Hölderlin wrote *Andenken* and *Der Ister* on the same page probably at about the same time in 1803/4. Heidegger claims that the former tells us something about the apparent backward flow of the Ister, its return to its origin in the East (*EHP* 107).

> He appears, however, almost
> To go backwards and
> I presume he must come from the East.
> There would be much to tell of this. (cited in *HH* 5)

Part III of the *Der Ister* lecture and the lecture on *Andenken* raise the notion of dwelling to a new level of interpretation. The central insight of both lectures is that the greeting *of* the foreigner, in both the subjective and the objective genitive, sets the poet on his journey from the Orient to the Occident. What makes possible dwelling in this instance is not the relation to the earth in holy mourning but, rather, the hospitality of the foreigner.

How does a thinking of hospitality arise in Heidegger? It arises largely owing to his use of Hölderlin's letter to Böhlendorff from 4 December 1801 in his reading of *Der Ister* and *Andenken*. That letter introduces a thinking of alterity in his reflections on dwelling.

The alterity of being in relation to beings appears in the guise of the alterity of the foreign or strange (*das Fremde*) in relation to the proper (*das Eigene*). The idea is that the Hesperian poet learns to dwell in what is proper to him, he appropriates what is natural to him as his appointed task, to the extent that the foreigner, the Greek poet of the heavenly fire, greets him in his dwelling. The foreigner is the unhomely one in the home. He does not simply point the Hesperian poet in the direction of the homely. In greeting the Hesperian poet, the foreigner calls him to his vocation as the sayer of the holy.

Hölderlin's first letter to Böhlendorff is usually read as giving an account of the difference between Greek and modern art against Winckelmann's neo-classicism and, more generally, against the way the issue is framed in the so-called quarrel of the ancients and the moderns. Should modern art imitate the superior and inimitable art of the Greeks and Romans? Is that the best the modern artist can hope for? Or has modern art far surpassed the art of the Classical Age?

Hölderlin displaces that entire debate by contesting its basic premises. He argues that the Greeks and moderns have nothing in common except for the 'living relationship and destiny' (Hölderlin, 1988: 150). The law of destiny is the formal principle that any culture or people, any community of language and memory that wants to appropriate what is proper to it must also learn what is foreign to it: it must be expropriated. Aside from that, the Greeks and moderns have nothing in common. Their art and culture (clarity of presentation) is a response to a nature (the holy pathos) that is foreign to ours, just as our art and culture (holy pathos) is a response to a nature (clarity of presentation) that is foreign to theirs. This invites the thought that history, far from being causal or linear, has a chiasmic structure (see Warminski, 1987 and Lacoue-Labarthe, 1989).

Heidegger is not unaware of Hölderlin's unique relation to the Greeks. He recognizes that, for Hölderlin, the Greek world is neither a model that we moderns ought to imitate – say, the model of a naivety and innocence, of a proximity to nature, as Schiller claims in *On Naïve and Sentimental Poetry*, that we should yearn for or aspire to return to – nor is it of the same essence and historical determination as ours. Hölderlin's relation to the Greeks, Heidegger writes, is 'neither classical, nor romantic, nor metaphysical' (*HH* 54).

However, Heidegger's use of the letter in his reading of Hölderlin's later hymns departs from the usual reading in at least two ways. As I mentioned above, the letter is usually read as Hölderlin's mature account of the difference between Greek and modern art. Heidegger sees it as a reflection on the content of what is poetized in the later hymns. That is the becoming homely of Hesperia (*HH* 124).

More significantly for my purpose here, Heidegger departs from the usual reading of the foreign of Hesperia, the 'heavenly fire' or 'holy pathos'. Paul de Man (2012) suggests that what is foreign to Hesperia is the nostalgic longing for the mystical unification with Nature that is characteristic of early Romanticism and that the narrator of *Hyperion* expresses in the opening letters of the novel, what Lacoue-Labarthe calls the 'transgression of finitude'. On that reading, Hölderlin says in his letter to Böhlendorff that a confrontation with that longing for unity is necessary if we are to learn to make a free use of what is proper to us, the clarity of presentation, and, as a result, if we are to produce a properly Hesperian art.

On Heidegger's reading, the foreign element that makes possible the free use of what is properly Hesperian (the clarity of presentation) is being. He refers to the latter with various expressions in the *Der Ister* lecture, 'the overwhelming', 'the uncanny', 'the ungraspable'.

> What is thus 'inborn' cannot properly become what is their own for the Germans so long as this ability to grasp (*Fassenkönnen*) has not been made to confront the necessity of grasping the ungraspable (*das Unfassliche zu fassen*) and of grasping themselves in the face of what is ungraspable. (*HH* 136)

Thought flourishes, it learns to dwell in its element, when it is made to confront the limit of thought. That is the light that illuminates entities but that cannot in turn be grasped as an entity.

That encounter with what is foreign to thought is the necessary condition of possibility for a particular Hesperian humanity, 'the Germans' – a word whose nominal unity Heidegger does not take for granted, I believe, inasmuch as it denotes not the Germans of 1942 but a non-extant people, a community to come – to appropriate what is 'inborn' to it as its historical vocation.

7. Guestfriendship

How is the encounter between the proper and the foreign to be understood? *Der Ister* describes it as a relation of hospitality and friendship, of guestfriendship.

> Thus it surprises
> Me not, that he [the Ister]
> Invited Hercules as guest (*zu Gaste geladen*). (cited in *HH* 5)

Who or what is a guest? Heidegger explains:

> *Gast ist derjenige Fremde, der in einem ihm fremden Heimischen zeitweise heimisch wird und damit selbst sein Heimisches in das fremde Heimische bringt und von diesem aufgenommen wird.*

> A guest is that foreigner who for a time becomes homely in a foreign home
> and who brings what is homely for him in the foreign home and who is received
> in the foreign home. (*HH* 140–1)

The guest is a foreigner who brings what is proper to her in the home that has
given her hospitality. Heidegger continues:

> *In dieser Gastlichkeit der Ister liegt die Bereitschaft der Anerkennung des Fremden
> und seiner Fremde* … In this hospitality on the part of the Ister there lies the
> readiness to acknowledge the foreigner and his foreignness, that is, the fire
> from heaven that the Germans lack. *In der Gastfreundschaft liegt aber zugleich
> die Entschiedenheit, das Eigene als das Eigene nicht mit der Fremde zu mischen,
> sondern den Fremden sein zu lassen, der er ist.* But in guestfriendship there also
> lies the resolve not to mix the proper *qua* proper with the foreign but to let the
> foreigner be such as he is. Only so is a learning possible in guestfriendship, namely
> a learning of what the calling and essence of the German poet is. (*HH* 141)

Let me recall that these sentences, which emphatically stress the priority of the
foreigner and her foreignness over the proper and the homely – indeed, as the
very condition of possibility of the revelation of the proper of the 'Germans' – were
written in 1942, at the time when the extermination camps in Poland had just
opened. Of course, the foreigner who is invited as guest by the Hesperian poet is
not the expelled, the converted, the assimilated or the exterminated. It is the Greek
poet of the heavenly fire. As Judith Butler (2009) says in *Frames of War: When Is
Life Grievable?*, some lives are just not grievable. Their loss goes unrecognized.

In what sense, however, is the foreigner foreign or strange? Is the stranger a
foreigner on the ground that her nationality, gender or race is other than that of
the Hesperian poet? That is doubtless not what Heidegger has in mind. The poet
of the heavenly fire is not foreign to the Hesperian poet because the first is Greek
and the second, German.

Heidegger casts being, the foreign fire, and the holy in the figure of the foreign
guest and stranger in the *Der Ister* lecture. Now what is proper to that stranger?

That stranger does not bear *strangeness* as an extrinsic quality. It defines her
very content or essence. That means that such a stranger is not identifiable as
an entity, whether as a person or thing, a who or what, as if we could know in
advance what she is or where she is. Singular in the extreme, already there and
yet to come, she defies classification and localization.

Already there as guest in my world, the stranger constitutes its absolute limit,
the limit of the becoming-mine of Dasein. Isn't that why the stranger introduces

the possibility of frenzy and madness, of an absolute disorientation and loss of self in one's home or nation?

Perhaps that is why the stranger sometimes passes for a god or monster, and why a sacrificial logic is most often deployed against her, the logic of the scapegoat, as Richard Kearney explains it in *Strangers, Gods and Monsters.*[6]

It is, in any case, what authorizes Jean-François Lyotard to ask how Heidegger's thought, 'a thought so devoted to remembering that a forgetting (of Being) takes place in all thought', could possibly 'have ignored the thought of "the jews," which, in a certain sense, thinks, tries to think, nothing but that very fact' (Lyotard, 1997: 4).

In der Gastfreundschaft liegt aber zugleich die Entschiedenheit, das Eigene als das Eigene nicht mit der Fremde zu mischen, sondern den Fremden sein zu lassen, der er ist. In guestfriendship, the host seeks neither to protect what is proper to him nor to appropriate the property of the foreigner. To be hospitable is to be open to the foreigner in her foreignness without reservation and without conditions imposed on her, such as that she declare her name, show her papers, speak the local language, and so on. It is be resolutely open to the distance that separates the self and the other in her alterity.

The relation to the foreigner, Heidegger adds, is never a mere taking-over, an assumption or appropriation of the other (*bloße Übernehmen des Anderen*). The relation to the proper is never a self-assured affirmation of the so-called *natural* or *organic* (*selbstsichere Bejahung des sogenannten 'Natürlichen' und 'Organischen'*) (*HH* 143). To be hospitable is to let the stranger be as she is in her strangeness in one's home. It resembles the greeting Heidegger describes in his lecture on Hölderlin's *Andenken*.

> *Solches Wesenlassen eines Wesenden in seinem Wesen ist das ursprüngliche Grüßen.* This letting-be of a being in its being is the originary greeting. (*EHP* 128)

Heidegger remarks in the *Der Ister* lecture that the guest is the presence of the unhomely in the home (*die Gegenwart des Unheimischen im Heimischen*) and that she turns the thinking of the homely into a steadfast remembrance (*ständigen Andenken*) of the journey to the foreign. *Die Aneignung des Eigenen ist nur als die Auseinandersetzung und gastliche Zwiesprache mit dem Fremden.* The appropriation of the proper *is* only as the encounter and guest-like conversation with the foreign. (*HH* 142) The foreigner does not cease to be foreign in this conversation, as if she was becoming less and less strange to the Hesperian poet in the course of it. Nor does this conversation reach a *terminus ad quem*, as if, having appropriated what is proper to him, the Hesperian poet could now dispense with and forget about his foreign guest, expel her from his home.

The Hesperian poet comes to appropriate his vocation in and through the continued dialogue with the foreign guest. The guest is not a means for the Hesperian poet to arrive at what is proper to him. The stranger is already there at the source as a guest (*schon an der Quelle das Fremde zu Gast und gegenwärtig ist*) (*HH* 146). She is the origin of the proper. To receive the stranger's greeting and thus enter in conversation with her is what constitutes the free use of the proper of the Hesperian poet. The Hesperian poet does not first have a home in which to greet the stranger. The stranger's greeting is what first sets the Hesperian poet on the way home.

What are we to make of this greeting? In what sense does the greeting of the foreigner come first?

And yet, have we not in a sense always already been greeted in the irreplaceability of one's existence? Is that not why the first gesture of thought is not to question but to respond with thanks for this 'highest and most lasting gift given to us' (*WCT* 142)?

There is a certain semantic affinity between *remembrance* and *greeting* in the ordinary use of *Andenken* current in Hölderlin's time. Dieter Henrich explains:

> The word *Andenken* was commonly used in the sense of abiding thoughts and warm regards for a person or an event, though this sense soon became archaic. In letters one assured friends of one's remembrance and entrusted oneself to theirs in greetings and best wishes. (Henrich, 1997: 213)

Ordinarily, we greet someone whom we don't know or haven't seen in a while and in whose presence we are now standing. We are rejoiced at seeing them or at seeing them again. We also send our greetings and best wishes, as we do in an email, to someone in whose presence we are no longer or not yet standing. We entrust ourselves to them as their friend.

A greeting in that sense is a token of affection that is sent and received between friends. It highlights the distance that separates the sender and receiver. It also preserves their proximity or nearness in this distance. It does not, however, annul the distance.

A greeting breeds neither familiarity nor ingratiation (*Anbiederung*). *Der echt Gruß schenkt dem Gegrüßten den Anklang seines Wesens* (*EHP* 120). As the recipient of a greeting, I have been charged with the responsibility to respond.

Since that responsibility is non-transferable, the greeting singles me out in the irreplaceability of my existence. What is the proper response to a greeting? To return the greeting as someone greeted and welcomed in his essence.

> The greeting is a *remembrance* or *thinking-of* (An-denken) whose mysterious strength shelters again (*zurückbirgt*) the recipient and sender of the greeting in the distance of their proper essence (*das Gegrüßte und den Grüßenden in die Ferne ihres eigenen Wesens*). (*EHP* 120)

A true greeting is a pure gift. It is a disinterested gesture that wants nothing for itself. *Der Gruß will nichts für sich*. It is a relation to the other in her alterity or uniqueness.

The friendship instituted by the greeting is not a relation between individuals who are contemporaries or familiar with each other. It is a relation between the Hesperian poet and the foreign guest (the holy). The foreigner is present to the poet in her greeting to him or, what amounts to the same thing, in his remembrance of his journey abroad.[7]

However, the foreigner becomes a destiny for the poet insofar as the distance that separates them is not annulled. He must maintain a sober relation with her. Instead of a mystical unification with the foreigner, the poet must view her as a possibility to come. To appropriate his vocation, he must project that which has been as what is futural in the extreme. He must open Hesperian humanity to the possibility of the coming of the stranger, or the coming of the holy. That is 'sobriety for the sublime' (*EHP* 142).

What is the holy for Heidegger?

I don't think it refers to the unity of the most extreme opposites, as it apparently does for Hölderlin, the unity that heals the rupture and separation between man and the god, the finite and the infinite. Nor does it mean the demonic, that is, the confusion of the limits between the animal, the human and the gods, as it does for Jan Patočka (see Derrida, 1996: 2).

It doubtless has a plurality of senses in Heidegger's reflections between his first lecture on Hölderlin in 1934 and his thought in the 1950s on the fourfold. In the context of the lectures studied in this chapter, however, the holy is the correlate of holy mourning. It refers to the collapse of the divine as a historical possibility. That collapse is the experience of the retreat of the gods.

Acknowledging the distance that separates the human being and the gods, the poet preserves a proximity to them. Their greeting, stored in his remembrance, affects the poet as a silent voice, *die lautlose Stimme des Grußes* (*EHP* 146). It welcomes the poet into his poet-hood and calls him to his vocation as the sayer of the holy. That greeting summons the poet to build a house (*Haus*), that is, a poem, for the heavenly ones who are to come as guests (*Gast*).

> For only when this third element, *the guesthouse* (**das Gasthaus**), stands between the heavenly ones and men, is there a place of mortal preparedness for the nearness of the heavenly ones, so that the heavenly ones can be for us the ones who they are. (*EHP* 142)

The poet founds a home in which he will be able to recollect his journey abroad under the foreign fire on his way to his proper vocation. That home is the guesthouse for the gods, the modern or Hesperian poem.

As I argued in section 3, the gods to which the poet extends his hospitality do not denote a *who* or a *what*, a person or thing. They are not objects of worship and belief, of devotion and prayer, of a religious institution, cult or dogma. They are figurations of historical time, of a future that is through and through undecidable (*des Unentscheidbaren*) (*CP* 30).

In the end, we have to ask ourselves whether, instead of thinking of the gods as guests of a particular kind, Heidegger is rethinking the notion of the guest. If the guest is a stranger in my home who has something of the uncanny about him, if he is the index of an arrival and departure, of the limit that opens my home to the outside, then he is someone who belongs and does not belong to the home. He is both inside and outside, already there at the source and yet to come. The foreign guest, a figure of passage and transition, of passing away, both familiar and foreign, near and remote, the very figure of the threshold: he is the presence of the uncanny in the at-home of the host.

Beyond Truth

I also want to make asceticism natural again.
—Friedrich Nietzsche, *The Will to Power*

1. Introduction[1]

There are at least two opposed readings in the literature about the kind of figure that Nietzsche presents of himself as in his later works. There is *Nietzsche, the metaphysician of the will to power and the eternal return*, and there is *Nietzsche, the sceptic, the iconoclast and the destroyer of metaphysical systems and ideas*. Heidegger's reading is probably the strongest interpretation available in support of the former, whereas Derrida's presents a solid account of the latter.

The aim of this chapter is to provide an alternative to both of these antithetical readings. Contra Heidegger, I show that Nietzsche does not reject the notion of truth understood as the correctness of judgment on the ground of a metaphysical understanding of the world as chaos. Contra Derrida, I argue that Nietzsche does not abandon a commitment to the propositional notion of truth in favour of scepticism, irony, rhetoric or play.

Nietzsche neither rejects nor abandons the notion of truth. His critique of the will to truth involves a suspension of our endorsement of propositions in a manner similar to Husserl's suspension of the natural attitude. But rather than disclosing the transcendental field of constituting consciousness, that suspension in Nietzsche invites the reader to engage in a practice of self-constitution in relation to the tragic insight that the propositions that we have thus far accepted as true are based on errors.

What Nietzsche proposes, I argue, is a new practice of self-discipline. Its aim is not merely to neutralize metaphysical characterizations of the world, whether as being or as becoming, as reality or as appearance. Its aim is to incorporate the insight that the totality of propositions that has defined Western humanity's self-understanding since Plato rests on simplifications, errors or fictions. The principal question here is not *Is that insight true?* but, rather, *What would that insight do to me, how would it transform me, if it were true?* and *Am I able to overcome the resistances to it?* In Nietzsche's eyes, what remains at the end of metaphysics, once the distinction between the supersensuous and the sensuous worlds has collapsed in the general insight that our most cherished and prized truths rest on illusions, is a practice that uses these so-called truths as means and tests of self-overcoming. Nietzsche is, like Heidegger, a thinker of the limit of metaphysics.

In section 2, I lay out Heidegger's argument against Nietzsche in two texts written in the 1930s, *Plato's Doctrine of Truth* (1931/2) and *The Will to Power as Knowledge* (1939). Heidegger's argument is that, appearances notwithstanding, Nietzsche does not abandon the notion of truth as correspondence. Nietzsche rejects the commonsensical notion of propositional truth (truth is a property of propositions) on the ground that propositions cannot be in harmony with reality since the former have unchanging logical and categorial forms whereas reality has the character of chaos. Since harmony with reality is a kind of correspondence, Nietzsche's rejection of propositional truth is based on his commitment to a certain understanding of correspondence.

In section 3, I explain that to be in harmony with reality for Heidegger/ Nietzsche consists in a way of life called *justice*. Its aim is to construct a world of re-identifiable objects that will afford the embodied subject the means to secure its identity and permanence.

In section 4, I note an ambiguity in Heidegger's reading and show that *Nietzsche, the sceptic and naturalist* remains an undeveloped aspect of Heidegger's interpretation. In section 5, I explain in what sense Nietzsche's thought constitutes the end of metaphysics for Heidegger and the way Heidegger proposes to defeat the anthropocentrism and anthropomorphism of late modernity.

In sections 6 and 7, I propose the alternative reading of Nietzsche briefly sketched in this introduction. In section 8, I consider whether Nietzsche's practice of self-discipline presupposes, as a necessary condition of possibility, the forgottenness of being.

2. Truth and error

In this section, I explain Heidegger's argument against Nietzsche in the 1930s, namely that Nietzsche remains committed to a certain understanding of truth as correspondence in spite of his apparent rejection of it. In section 3, I clarify the sense in which that correspondence must be taken in Heidegger/Nietzsche. Then, in section 4, I turn to highlight an ambiguity in Heidegger's reading of Nietzsche before I present an alternative interpretation of Nietzsche on truth in sections 6, 7 and 8.

In section 5, I address what is doubtless the most contentious point in Heidegger's reading of Nietzsche. That is his charge that Nietzsche anthropomorphizes the world. I argue that there are good reasons for thinking that Heidegger's charge sticks.

* * *

In a note dated 1885, Nietzsche writes:

> *Truth is the kind of error* without which a particular kind of living creature could not live. The value for life is what ultimately decides. (Nietzsche, 2003: 16)

Heidegger cites this note in the final paragraphs of *Plato's Doctrine of Truth*. He then comments:

> If for Nietzsche truth is a kind of error, then its essence consists in a way of thinking that always, indeed necessarily falsifies the real, specifically insofar as every act of representing halts the continual 'becoming' and, in erecting its established facts against the flow of 'becoming', sets up as the supposedly real something that does not correspond – i.e. something incorrect and thus erroneous.
>
> Nietzsche's determination of truth as the incorrectness of thinking is in agreement with the traditional essence of truth as the correctness of assertion (*logos*). (*PM* 179)

Let me begin by clarifying what Heidegger means in the passage by reference to how truth is usually thought.

Truth is ordinarily understood in two ways. Aristotle, Aquinas and others speak of truth in relation to what exists and in relation to propositions. We say, for instance, *that is how things are in truth* or *things are in truth like that*. What is meant by such phrases is that things have certain characteristics or properties that do not depend on the way we think or interact with them and that these characteristics are unchanging and self-identifying. What is meant is that they behave just as the world of being behaves in Plato. Truth in this metaphysically realist sense refers to what exists in itself and, correlatively, to what is transparent to the mind.[2]

Truth is also thought in relation to propositions. In this context, it is the property of the propositional content of a declarative sentence. Truth signifies the agreement of a proposition with what exists in itself.

The expression *truth* in Nietzsche's assertion that *truth is a kind of error* can thus mean the following:

a. There is a world that exists in itself.
b. Truth is the property of a proposition.

Conversely, *error* can mean two things as well. As a predicate that describes how things are in themselves, it carries the sense of the unstable, the impermanent, the different, chaos or becoming. To say of the world that the only kind of power that rules in it is the 'power of the false' (Deleuze) is not to remove something positive from the world. It is not to add something negative to it. It is to give the world a positive metaphysical interpretation as a world of becoming.

So, for example, the body for Nietzsche represents our indelible encounter with chaos. Chaos, Heidegger explains in *The Will to Power as Knowledge*, is not the confused or the unordered. It is what urges and flows. It is what is animated. It is the stream of life whose order remains hidden.

> Chaos is the name for bodying life, life as bodying writ large. (*N3* 80)

Nietzsche says in a note from his late notebooks that the body is not a thing in which qualities or forces inhere. The word *body* designates a dynamic interaction of forces (Nietzsche, 2003: 30). He insists that the body in that precise sense must be made the basis and guideline for the interpretation of the world.

What does *error* mean as the property of a proposition from the standpoint of the interpretation of the world as becoming?

Error in this context cannot simply mean that a proposition is not in agreement with the facts. According to the first two classical laws of thought, a proposition cannot represent anything unless it represents it as something that is identical (x is x) and non-contradictory (I cannot represent x as x and as non-x at the same time and in the same respect). If the world has the character of becoming, then the representational content of a proposition that conforms to the laws of thought will falsify the world.

Error thus means falsification, simplification, construction or creation. The representational content of a proposition arrests the flow of becoming in logical and categorial forms. That makes it possible to represent the world and talk about it (*N3* 95, 107, 116).

Nietzsche's assertion that truth is a kind of error can consequently mean the following:

c. The world as it exists in itself is not a world of being but a world of becoming.

d. A proposition (owing to its logical and categorial forms) falsifies what exists in itself.

Now Heidegger argues that Nietzsche rejects b., the propositional notion of truth, on the ground of the metaphysical interpretation of the world in c. For Nietzsche, the propositional notion of truth falsifies the real because it is *not in harmony with the real*, which is in flux. *Harmony with the real* is the metaphysical standard in relation to which the propositional notion of truth is challenged. But harmony with the real is a form of correspondence. Accordingly, Nietzsche's rejection of the propositional notion of truth is based on his commitment to the correspondence theory.

Heidegger writes in *The Will to Power as Knowledge* that Nietzsche's assertion that truth is a kind of error thinks truth twice:

> And each time differently, hence ambiguously: once as fixation of the constant [in a propositional content], and then as harmony with the actual. Only on the basis of this essence of truth as harmony can truth as constancy be an error. The essence of truth here underlying the concept of error is what has been determined since ancient times in metaphysical thinking as correspondence with the actual and harmony with it, *homoiosis*. (N3 126)

How is that harmony with reality to be understood?

3. Justice

Harmony with reality is not to be taken in the sense of the copy-model relation. It is not as if Nietzsche is saying that changes in the world cause replicas of themselves in the mind. What Heidegger seems to have in mind is something like the ethical idea of the Stoics of living *in accordance with* nature. That comes out in his discussion of knowledge, art and justice in *The Will to Power as Knowledge*.

Knowledge and art are, for Nietzsche, enabling conditions of human life. They are conditions under which a stable environment is secured against chaos.

Nietzsche says in a note that '[e]very belief is a holding-to-be-true' (Nietzsche, 2003: 149). If I believe *that the cat is on the mat* then I believe that it is true *that the cat is on the mat*. To believe for Nietzsche is to endorse a proposition. It is to accept it as true.

Heidegger reads that passage differently. Thing-hood, inherence, causality and so on are categorial forms built in a propositional content or representation in general. Now to endorse a proposition presupposes as a necessary condition of possibility the unity of self-awareness, the identity of the *I think*. The identity of the subject presupposes, in turn, as a necessary condition of possibility, the identity of the object, that is, a referent that is re-identifiable as the same over time and that constitutes what the proposition is about. Heidegger claims, in this Kantian reading of Nietzsche, that to endorse a proposition presupposes the organization of the flux of stimuli in re-identifiable objects such as things, properties, causes and so on.

> The sensuous crowds and overwhelms *us* as rational living beings, as those beings who have always already been intent on making things identical without expressly carrying out such an intention. For only what is identical offers the guarantee of the same; only the same secures constancy, while making constant effects the securing of permanence. (*N3* 98)

The chaos of sensations is not something that stands over against us. We 'ourselves, as bodily beings, are it' (*N3* 79). That implies that the aim of knowledge is not truth. It is to construct and endow the body of the living being with a stable structure and identity. To that end, a world of objects must be constituted by means of reason and its categories. Objects that are re-identifiable as the same afford living beings the possibility of securing their identity and permanence over time.

On Heidegger's reading, Nietzsche is a fictionalist about truth and the categories of reason. Knowledge and truth are resources and conditions of human life. They generate a world of being and superimpose it over a world of becoming. That makes possible the preservation of human life against the onslaught of becoming both from within and from without.

It is no different in the case of art. By art, Heidegger does not mean works of different genres.

> Art is the name for every form of transfiguring and viable transposition of life to higher possibilities. (*N3* 126)

By art, Heidegger means the drive in human life that produces sensuous appearances. Knowledge is a condition under which chaos is mastered in a constructed world of objects for a bodily subject. Like dreams are to reality, so is art the condition under which this construct of knowledge is transfigured into an aesthetic construct, a higher possibility of mastering chaos.

Like knowledge, art arrests the flow of becoming in sensuous appearances. But what it presents is not constrained by the limits of knowledge. That is why art offers human life unanticipated possibilities of self- and world-mastery.

Accordingly, art and knowledge are devoted to the same vital activity.

> *Art and knowledge in their reciprocity first bring about the full securing of permanence of the animate as such....* . [B]oth are in essence one: namely, the assimilation and the direction of human life to chaos, *homoiosis*. Such assimilation is not imitative and reproductive adaptation to something at hand, but *transfiguration that commands and poetizes, establishes perspectival horizons, and fixates*. (N3 140)

That assimilation to chaos is the norm the living being uses to produce stable constructs of domination. That assimilation is what Nietzsche has in mind, according to Heidegger, when he speaks of *Gerechtigkeit*, rightness or justice, in a note written in 1884.[3]

> *Justice* as a constructive, exclusive, annihilative mode of thought, arising from estimations of value: *The supreme representative of life itself.*

Heidegger hears in Nietzsche's word an echo of the metaphysical notion of *Richtigkeit*, of truth as correctness.

Heidegger's reading here must be taken with caution. That note on justice antedates by a year the first mention of the will to power in Nietzsche's notebooks (see Nietzsche, 2003: 15) and its first published use by two years in *Beyond Good and Evil* (1886). In spite of that, justice in Heidegger's eyes embodies the essence of power.

> This way of thinking [i.e., justice] is a self-surpassing, a becoming master of oneself from having climbed and opened a higher height. We call such self-surpassing heightening *overpowering*. It is the essence of power. (N3 146)

The essence of power consists in a mode of thought that approaches science, art, politics and religion from a perspective that is beyond good and evil. It is a mode of thought for which these practices are conditions of human life. It recognizes these practices as conditions that both preserve human life in the face of chaos and change and that enhance and intensify it by making use of chaos to its own ends.

Justice in this sense, Heidegger writes, is 'the ground of the possibility and necessity of every kind of harmony of man with chaos' (N3 149). To be in harmony with chaos does not mean to be in accord with the facts. It is a way of life that consists in stabilizing chaos in constructs of domination. It is a way of life that aims at self- and world-mastery.

That is why it requires the thought of the eternal return of chaos. It is its greatest antithesis and it is only against that obstacle that this way of life, justice, can flourish. Nietzsche writes in a note that Heidegger cites:

> Life itself created the thought which is most burdensome for life; it wants to *surpass* its greatest obstacle! (*N3* 214)

Justice is a mode of thought and a way of life that posits its own greatest obstacle – the thought of the eternal return of chaos – to surpass itself and overcome the levels of stabilization it designs. In learning to master itself and the world against that obstacle, the will to power 'is continually under way toward its essence. It is eternally active and must at the same time be end-less' (*N3* 210).[4]

4. Naturalism

I explained in section 2 Heidegger's argument against Nietzsche, his claim, namely, that Nietzsche's rejection of the correspondence theory is merely apparent and is based on a commitment to an understanding of it as harmony with reality. In section 3, I explained what that harmony with reality amounts to. In this section, I highlight an ambiguity in Heidegger's reading. Heidegger presents Nietzsche as an idealist and naturalist. In addition, *Nietzsche, the sceptic and naturalist* remains undeveloped in Heidegger's interpretation.

In the next section, I turn to the most controversial aspect of Heidegger's reading. That is his reading of Nietzsche as anthropomorphizing the world. I argue that this reading is not without justification.

* * *

There is a notable ambiguity in Heidegger's presentation of Nietzsche in *The Will to Power as Knowledge* and in *European Nihilism*, the lecture delivered the year after in 1940.

On the one hand, Heidegger casts Nietzsche as the last great idealist of the German philosophical tradition starting with Kant. Nietzsche is seen as someone who believes that the immutable world of speculative and moral facts, Truth with a capital letter, is a value posited by and for human life and that this world has, in consequence, no veritable mind-independent reality.

That is how Heidegger aims to protect Nietzsche from naturalizing and biologizing readers like Alfred Baeumler and other Nazi ideologues. For instance,

Heidegger says that against the realist notion of truth as 'copying and imitating something at hand', Nietzsche opposes 'the nature of positing, poetizing, and commanding'. Heidegger adds two pages later:

> Nietzsche thinks the 'biological', the essence of what is alive, in the direction of commanding and poetizing, of the perspectival and horizonal: in the direction of freedom. (*N3* 120, 122)

Freedom has here the Kantian sense of self-determination. Heidegger wants to say that Nietzsche completes Kant's critique of theocentric metaphysics by ensconcing himself more deeply than anyone before him in an anthropocentric metaphysics.

> So little is Nietzsche's thinking in danger of biologism that on the contrary he rather tends to interpret what is biological in the true and strict sense – the plant and animal – *nonbiologically*, that is, *humanly*. (*N3* 122)

On the other hand, however, Heidegger does not deny Nietzsche's naturalist thrust against idealism.[5] Heidegger's reading of art and knowledge as conditions of human life places Nietzsche squarely in the context of evolutionary epistemology and aesthetics.

Besides, as we have seen, Heidegger does not underplay Nietzsche's talk of life as chaos and of chaos as 'the name for bodying life', of 'life as bodying writ large'. Or again, Heidegger refers to Nietzsche's inversion of the pre-eminence of reason to the pre-eminence of the body in section 22 of *European Nihilism* titled *The End of Metaphysics*.

What would *the end of metaphysics* signify from the standpoint of Nietzsche as naturalist?

No doubt, it would signify the end of idealism, that is, the devaluation of the value ascribed to man in modernity as the focal point around which the world is organized, as the subject for which there is a world, as the legislator of the norms of truth, goodness and beauty, as the *telos* of history and progress – in short, the devaluation of all those ways of thinking that posit the human being at the centre of things and that are, accordingly, anthropocentric.

That devaluation is hinted at in the way Nietzsche's discourse imperceptibly moves from talking about *human life* to talking about *life in general*. In that move, the human being, conceived as a rational animal, as a body endowed with a soul and spirit, and thus granted infinite value, disappears. It reappears as a finite mode connected with an infinity of other finite modes, each of which constitutes a perspectival variation on a singular cosmic force, the will to power.

How is the propositional notion of truth as error and as a falsification of life to be understood from this angle, if this falsification can no longer be seen as the result of a human agency, if *human agency* must, in turn, be seen as an error and falsification of life? *Who* or *what* falsifies life?

Nietzsche writes in a note dated 1885:

> 'Truth': in my way of thinking that does not necessarily mean an antithesis of error, but in the most fundamental cases only the relative position of various errors. (Nietzsche, 2003: 35)

Truth is thought as the antithesis of error in the principle of bivalence. By denying that, Nietzsche denies that there is a literal or strict sense to the words *truth* and *error*. Isn't *that* Nietzsche's ultimate post-metaphysical and anti-idealist gesture, that is, to reduce the idea of error to a metaphor, to an image for a world without vertical antitheses and ontological hierarchies, a world without distinction between high and low, good and evil, God, man and animal?

Heidegger does not appear to acknowledge that aspect of Nietzsche's thought. He seems to take Nietzsche far too literally and far too seriously. Nietzsche's playfulness is conspicuously absent in his reading. Nietzsche remains a metaphysician in Heidegger's eyes, indeed, the last great metaphysician of the West.

5. The end of metaphysics

Heidegger interprets the way Nietzsche shifts from talking about *human life* to talking about *life in general* accordingly, that is, as establishing a metaphysical thesis rather than as a gesture that takes us beyond metaphysics and idealism.

> In Nietzsche's thinking *life* is usually the term for what is and for beings as a whole insofar as they are. Occasionally, however, it also means our life in a special sense, which is to say, the being of man. (*N3* 15)

Life interpreted as will to power signifies at least two things for Heidegger:

a. Anthropomorphism

It makes explicit the anthropomorphism that has been lying dormant since the beginning of modernity with Descartes who introduces self-consciousness as a basic condition of the knowledge of being.

Descartes argues in *Meditations on First Philosophy* that self-consciousness is the first principle in the order of knowledge. That means that human I-hood must be presupposed at the basis of the representation of the world.

Once the *I think* is posited as the ground of knowledge, the traditional concept of the subject, understood as a *support* or *underlying thing*, is restricted to human self-awareness. *To be a subject* henceforth means *to be a human agent*. And that, in turn, means to be the ground and first principle of knowledge and truth.

From that moment on, it is no longer possible to identify the ground of knowledge with truth in the divine intellect. The ground of knowledge is the human *I*, and that *I* is an entity that is identical to itself through time, that unifies its experiences and that is aware of doing so.

No doubt, that notion of subjectivity as agency does not come to light before the Kantian revolution. Descartes has a contemplative rather than a constitutive model of awareness. Nevertheless, Heidegger sees it as anticipated by Descartes's notion of the *Cogito*.

> The consciousness of things and objects is essentially and in its ground primarily self-consciousness; only as self-consciousness is consciousness of ob-jects possible. For representation as described, the *self* of man is essential as what lies at the very ground. The self is *sub-iectum*. (*N4* 108)

The mind is a basic condition of the knowledge of being in Descartes. It becomes a basic condition of being in Leibniz. Being is conceived not only as representation and perception but also as striving or effort (*conatus seu nisus*), a striving to exist, to become actual and effective. With Leibniz, subjectivity is for the first time introduced as a constituent feature of being.

That is the historical setting that makes possible assertions in Nietzsche such as a 'quantum of force is equivalent to a quantum of drive, will, effect – more, it is nothing other than precisely this very driving, willing, effecting' (Nietzsche, 1989: 45).

Does that interpretation of force as will in Nietzsche invite an understanding of the world in the image of the human being, such that anything that lives is now seen as driving, willing or effecting?

It can hardly be doubted that Nietzsche's discourse unsettles the received interpretations of the human being. In fact, his aim in *The Gay Science* is to remove all human projections and anthropomorphisms from nature and '*naturalize* humanity with a pure, newly discovered, newly redeemed nature' (Nietzsche, 2008: 110). What reason could Heidegger have for saying that

Nietzsche's discourse seeks 'the true and the real in the *absolute humanization* of all beings' (*N4* 83)?

As Heidegger sees it – and, I think, he's right about this – anthropomorphism (the world posited in the image of man) and anthropocentrism (man posited at the centre of the world) do not result from ascribing to the human being an exorbitant value. It follows, conversely, that it is naïve to think that anthropomorphism and anthropocentrism can be removed from the world simply by reducing the value of the human being to nil in an unbounded nihilism or, what amounts to the same thing, in a doctrine of scientific materialism, as in Ray Brassier (2007) for example.

Anthropomorphism and anthropocentrism are offshoots of the modern understanding of being as subjectivity. If *to be* is to be *an object for a subject*, and the human being is the subject *par excellence* (on the ground that the self-consciousness of the human being is the foundation and first principle in the order of knowledge), then it is not surprising that we have been witnessing, since the Kantian revolution, the rise of an unrestrained anthropomorphism, of worldview philosophies that posit the human being at the centre of things and, more generally, of philosophies of the human subject.[6]

That is why Nietzsche's discourse is not critical enough. On what basis is the concept of the subject restricted to the self of the human being?[7] What makes possible the interpretation of being as subjectivity (the forgottenness of being)? Nietzsche does not ask these questions. The alterity of being in relation to entities remains unthought. That unthought constitutes the limit of his discourse. His discourse speaks from it and on the basis of it.

b. Value thinking

Heidegger also understands the will to power in Nietzsche as a principle of evaluation that arises once the distinction between the supersensuous and the sensuous worlds has collapsed and fallen to the ground. That principle interprets all that exists as conditions of human life.

These conditions are of two kinds. They either preserve human life against the onslaught of chaos or they enhance its mastery over chaos. In both cases, all that exists is made tangible as a value that preserves or fosters human life.

That is what Heidegger has in mind by the *end* of metaphysics in *European Nihilism*. Nietzsche does not spell its demise. The interpretation of all that exists as will to power means that a particular kind of thinking comes to dominate as the sole and exclusive thinking about the world. It is a thinking that is through and through human-centred. It perceives anything that exists as a value that serves to preserve or improve the biological and social existence of the human being. It is a thinking that is set on managing the human being and the world understood as a vast network of resources.

Metaphysics *completes itself* in that thinking in antithetical senses of the word. That completion, in other words, is Janus-faced:

1. On the one hand, it means that the forgottenness of being finds its first and lasting expression in the belief that there is nothing to the word *being*. As Nietzsche puts it, being is 'the last wisp of evaporating reality'. An age whose thinking and activities are centred on the human being believes that the word *being* is without meaning. That lack of meaning, moreover, does not perplex us. The fact that we do not have a clear understanding of what that word signifies does not distress us. It leaves us indifferent.[8] That indifference is something that is, in turn, forgotten.

That is what Heidegger means by nihilism. It does not mean the devaluation of the uppermost values as in Nietzsche. It defines an age in which there is nothing to being.

2. Metaphysics completes itself in the thought that *there is nothing to being*. A reflection on that thought, however, can awaken another kind of thinking beyond nihilism and value thinking. The completion of metaphysics also points in the direction of what Heidegger calls *meditative thinking* in the *Discourse on Thinking*.

The thought that *there is nothing to being* or that *being is without meaning* can be rephrased this way: *being is nothing*. No doubt, that phrase can be interpreted in a number of ways.

One way to interpret it is as follows. The terms that we use to describe entities cannot be used to describe being. Understanding it this way, we advert to the fact that being is other than entities.

Let us assume, in addition, that entities are made intelligible and manifest by reference to the present and its modalities (see Chapter 3.2). It follows that being, which is distinct from entities, cannot be understood by reference to a modality of the present. The alterity of being in relation to entities is the alterity of a past or future in relation to the present. In order to think of that alterity, we must cease thinking with the traditional predicates of being, since they are modifications of presence and are designed to think entities.

That is what Heidegger attempts to do in an essay written in 1944/6, *Nihilism as Determined by the History of Being*. Being, understood as the appearing of entities, is approached with a new vocabulary. It is conceived as a promise (*Versprechen*), as an absence (*Ausbleiben*), or as a secret (*Geheimnis*).

Three consequences follow from all this:

(a)   The reflection on being as nothing calls into question the modern understanding of being as subjectivity and, more broadly, the understanding of being as presence or actuality.

The Classical Greek notion of being as presence, and its subsequent interpretations in the history of Western thought up to and including Nietzsche's thought of the eternal return and will to power, feeds on the confusion between being and entities. To think being as nothing is the first step towards recognizing the difference between being and entities. It is to think being as singularity, that is, as an event that is without precedent in the totality of entities. It is to think at the limit of Western thought.

(b)   That reflection thinks the world, beyond anthropomorphism and anthropocentrism, by reference to the being of entities. It calls into question the idea that the human being is the zero-point, the centre of orientation or the origin of meaning of the world.
(c)   That reflection thinks the human Dasein, beyond its traditional notion as the rational animal, as an ecstatic openness that shelters being in an entity.

Sein ist Schein. Being signifies appearing, coming-to-presence, *Anwesen*. It is the light that suddenly breaks into entities. It differentiates them against each other and makes them visible in their outline and contours. It articulates their intelligibility through a play of contrast and difference. But that light is not itself an entity. It has neither contour nor outline that would enable us to describe it against something else.

Exposure to that light, if that were possible, would be exposure to nothingness, anxiety, death or loss of self. Language and meaning would fail in such an experience. Entities would lose their outline and contour. They would press upon the human Dasein in their entirety in their undifferentiated presence. All that would remain tangible is the sheer fact *that they are*.

That is why the veil is necessary. Being hides and shelters itself in entities so that the human Dasein can speak with others about things. Put differently, that light is manifest to the human Dasein as an absence or lack in the midst of entities that can be neither suppressed nor filled.

Heidegger identifies that lack with distress (*Not*) in *Nihilism as Determined by the History of Being* (*N4* 244). It is a distress that remains in reserve beyond the present.

Far from being reducible to a conscious state, distress is always already there in an anteriority that is more ancient than the first wakeful state of the human Dasein. It constitutes a throwness that cannot be retrieved in a project or it lies ahead of every project as the limit of the possible, as the possibility of the impossible. Like a trauma, it resists language, meaning and presence.

In sum, that reflection on being as nothing with these three consequences prepares and anticipates meditative thinking for Heidegger. The latter is a thinking that dwells 'on what lies close' and 'what is closest', 'upon that which concerns us, each one of us, here and now; here, on this patch of home ground; now, in the present hour of history' (*DT* 47). It prepares a thinking of the fourfold with the idea of being as an absence or lack in the midst of entities, that is, with the idea of *the thing* that gathers together the four folds of the world, the gods, the mortals, the sky and the earth.

6. The will to truth

I showed in section 2 that Heidegger contends that Nietzsche rejects the notion of truth as correctness of representation on the ground of a positive metaphysical interpretation of the world as a world of becoming. Propositions cannot be in harmony with the character of the world as chaos owing to their logical and categorial forms, which are unchanging. In consequence, we must reject the notion of correspondence that pertains to the truth of propositions. But harmony with the real is a type of correspondence. So Nietzsche's rejection of truth as correctness is a function of his commitment to a certain understanding of truth as correspondence.

Heidegger cashes out that idea of harmony with chaos as a way of life called justice. It is a way of life that aims to construct a world of re-identifiable objects so that the embodied subject can secure its identity and permanence in the face of the eternal return of chaos.

The problem with Heidegger's reading is, I think, that it is too coherent or too systematic. It focuses solely on *Nietzsche, the metaphysician and system builder*, the heir of Spinoza or Leibniz, at the expense of other possible, and doubtless contradicting, figures in Nietzsche's text.

Derrida *et alia* have stressed, against Heidegger's reading of Nietzsche as a metaphysician of the will to power and the eternal return, the element of play, irony and rhetoric as another strategy that Nietzsche deploys to deal with our commitment to truth (see Derrida, 1979).

The problem with Derrida's reading is its excessive focus on play and irony, on *Nietzsche, the sceptic, the iconoclast, the destroyer of metaphysical systems and ideas.* It makes Nietzsche out to be a thinker devoid of a substantive philosophical project.

In the next section, I intend to propose a different reading of Nietzsche that steers clear of both of these two extremes. I believe that Heidegger is wrong to think that Nietzsche *must* be committed to b. and c. in section 2, namely, that there is a world that exists in itself and that this world has the character of becoming, in order to reject the propositional notion of truth as correctness. That is not to say that this rejection must then follow from a sceptical attitude, that is, an attitude of irony and playfulness.

As I see it, Nietzsche's critique of the will to truth, in works published after *Beyond Good and Evil* (1886), particularly in *On the Genealogy of Morals* (1887) and *Twilight of the Idols* (1888), involves a suspension of our commitment to truth in a manner similar to Husserl's notion of the suspension of the natural attitude. However, that suspension in Nietzsche does not disclose the transcendental field of constituting consciousness. It invites the reader to engage in a practice of self-constitution before the tragic insight that the meaning and value of the world rests on irremovable errors. That is the new type of ascesis of the will that Nietzsche is looking for beyond the ascetic ideal and nihilism in his final works.

Contra Heidegger, Nietzsche does not reject the propositional notion of truth as correctness on the basis of a metaphysical understanding of the world as will to power. He asks his reader to suspend her natural commitment to truth. To neutralize that commitment also entails the suspension of metaphysics. It prohibits us from accepting as true any characterization of the world, including any way of life that aims and claims to be in harmony with reality.

Nietzsche is not left without a substantive philosophical project in the absence of a metaphysical thesis about the world. In Nietzsche's eyes, what remains once metaphysics and idealism are suspended is a project of self-fashioning and self-overcoming. That is what I intend to show in the next section. In section 8, I consider whether that project presupposes as a necessary condition of possibility the forgottenness of being.

7. Self-discipline

What is the ascetic ideal? It is a practice in which the self denies its earthly life for the sake of eternal happiness, or in which it seeks freedom from earthly pain and misery. In its undisguised form, the ascetic ideal is a practice of self-renunciation for the sake of what has unconditional worth, truth being the first of such things.

The three great slogans of the ascetic ideal, Nietzsche tells us, are poverty, humility and chastity (Nietzsche, 1989: 108). The ascetic man speaks of himself with nausea and pity, two emotions whose combination in a single will produces one of 'the uncanniest monsters: the "last will" of man, his will to nothingness: nihilism'. That man says to himself: ' "If only I were someone else" [. . .] "but there is no hope of that. I am who I am: how could I ever get free of myself? And yet – I *am sick of myself!*" ' (Nietzsche, 1989: 122) The ascetic man is the type of man who is not content with his lot and who copes with it by blaming himself for his discontentment (the ascetic priest turns the direction of *ressentiment* inwards: *it is my fault I suffer, not yours* [see Nietzsche, 1989: 127]).

Nietzsche dispels the illusion that modern science constitutes an antidote to the ascetic ideal. Science exposes man to a 'penetrating sense of his nothingness'. It forces him to denounce as an offence against scientific truth the belief in his dignity and absolute value, the belief in the freedom of his will as the sign of his noumenal nature. That '*will* to self-belittlement', that 'hard-worn *self-contempt* of man', has been the straightest route to 'the *old* ideal'.

Moreover, science's general renunciation of all interpretation – which is to say, of 'forcing, adjusting, abbreviating, omitting, padding, inventing, falsifying, and whatever else is of the *essence* of interpreting' – betrays as 'much ascetic ideal as any denial of sensuality'. What constrains the man of science is 'this unconditional will to truth, [which is his] *faith in the ascetic ideal itself* (Nietzsche, 1989: 151, 155–6).

Nietzsche concludes the Third Essay of *On the Genealogy of Morals* with the following task he assigns to his philosophy of the future.

> [Philosophers] are all oblivious of how much the will to truth itself first requires justification. [Because truth was posited as being, as God, as the highest court of appeal] truth was not *permitted* to be a problem at all.... From the moment faith in the God of the ascetic ideal is denied, a *new problem arises*: that of the *value* of truth.
>
> The will to truth requires a critique – let us thus define our own task – the value of truth must for once be experimentally *called into question*. (Nietzsche, 1989: 152–3)

What does it mean *to critique the will to truth* or to call the value of truth into question?

Nietzsche can be interpreted as saying that he is not attacking the concept of truth per se but only a particular meaning of it. Thus Maudemarie Clark argues that Nietzsche challenges the metaphysical notion of truth (correspondence with a thing-in-itself) but not the commonsensical notion of truth (correspondence of a statement with a state of affairs) (Clark, 1991: 30–1).

In contrast, Heidegger argues that Nietzsche challenges the commonsensical notion of truth but not the metaphysical one.

However, neither of these two proposals quite captures what Nietzsche has in mind in that passage.

No doubt, Nietzsche's emphasis is less on truth itself than on the *will* to truth or on its *value*. To question truth from the perspective of its value for life is to ask about the purpose for which we are committed to it: it is to bring into focus our natural and immediate trust in truth. That trust is both natural and immediate because it constitutes the very structure of belief and we are never without beliefs.

Every belief is a *holding-to-be-true*. (Nietzsche, 2003: 148)

There is no instance in which I believe that *p* but don't accept *p* as true. To subject my will to truth to a critique is to turn that structure into a theme. But that I cannot do unless I suspend every belief within me, that is, unless I choose to no longer participate in accepting-*p*-as-true. Nietzsche is not asking us to reject this or that theory of truth. If a belief by its nature purports to represent what is the case, then he is asking us to assume an attitude of neutrality with respect to what is the case.

It might be asked how that neutrality fits with Nietzsche's claim in a note written in 1881 where he says that we are 'to look into the world through as *many* eyes as possible, *to live* in drives and activities *so as* to create eyes for ourselves' (Ansell Pearson and Large, 2006: 239). That passage and its cousin in the *Genealogy* (see Nietzsche, 1989: 119) seems to suggest the contrary of what I am saying, namely, that Nietzsche is saying that we are to enter into and explore perspectives in order to know the world.

I am not sure that Nietzsche is interested in knowing what there is. After all, if neither the self nor the world has a nature that waits to be discovered, as Nietzsche believes, then there is nothing for us to know. What I take Nietzsche to be saying in the 1881 note is that perspectives, drives or passions are conditions of our human, all-too-human knowledge. To explore these perspectives, to enter into them is to expose the errors and simplifications on which our knowledge rests. My claim is that, in order to explore such perspectives and become attentive to the conditions of knowledge, we must assume an attitude of neutrality with regard to what our knowledge represents about the self or the world.

How else could Nietzsche claim to engage in a *critique* of the will to truth? For this critique to be *critical* rather than *dogmatic*, it must be immanent rather than transcendent. That means that it is not entitled to appeal to facts that are external to the will to truth, to such facts as that '*this world is the will to power – and nothing besides!*' (Nietzsche, 1968: 550). Nietzsche's critique precedes by right the assertion of any such fact.

Moreover, to assume an attitude of neutrality with regard to the representational content of propositions is by necessity to bring within the scope of one's critique all theories of truth, all beliefs about what truth might consist in, including metaphysical and commonsensical notions.

The problem with both Clark and Heidegger's readings is that they do not take seriously enough what it means for the reader to raise that question, what she is called upon to *do* in posing it: '*what is the meaning of all will to truth?*' If 'the will to truth thus gains self-consciousness' (Nietzsche, 1989: 161) as a problem, then that consciousness can no longer take that will for granted. It can no longer allow it to present facts about the world. Instead, it must subject to a critique the source of all truth-taking. That is the type of life that evaluates things as being thus-and-so in moral and cognitive practices.

Let me consider this from another angle. Nietzsche writes in *The Gay Science*:

> If we had not welcomed the arts and invented this kind of cult of the untrue, then the realization of general untruth and mendaciousness that now comes to us through science – the realization that delusion and error are conditions of human knowledge and sensation – would be utterly unbearable. (Nietzsche, 2008: 163)

The most extreme form of nihilism for Nietzsche arises not with the recognition that the world is meaningless (passive nihilism) but with the recognition that the meaning and value of life depend on fictions that we must accept as true (active nihilism). It arises with the general insight into error as a necessary condition of consciousness. Nietzsche continues in the note where he defines the structure of belief:

> The most extreme form of nihilism would be that *every* belief, every holding-to-be-true, is necessarily false: *because there is no **true world***. Thus: a *perspectival illusion* whose origins lie within us (inasmuch as we have a constant *need* of a narrower, abridged and simplified world)
>
> – that the ***measure of force*** is how far we can admit to ourselves illusoriness, the necessity of lies, without perishing.
>
> *To this extent nihilism, as the **denial** of a true world, of a being, might be a divine way of thinking.* (Nietzsche, 2003: 148–9)

Note that the focus in this and in the preceding passage of *The Gay Science* is not on the truth of that insight, but on how to endure it. That is highly significant. In submitting our will to truth to a critique, what Nietzsche is calling for is a revaluation of our attitude towards knowledge and truth. If we take deep pleasure and interest in deception and in being deceived in viewing a work of art, why can't we affirm the same pleasure and interest in viewing the errors and deceptions on which our conscious life rests?

Nietzsche is *not* committed to the paradoxical claim that *it is true that error is necessary*. Rather, he is committed to shifting the focus away from such metaphysical and epistemic questions as *Is error a character of how things are in themselves?* and *How can I know that?* to the ethical question *How can I live with that insight?*, or better, *What would that insight do to me, how would it affect and transform me, if I was to accept it as true?*

To place truth in the service of life, to ask about its value for life, is already to address truth from a post-metaphysical perspective. It is to address it from the perspective of a practice of self-discipline that uses its own will to truth as a test and means of self-overcoming.

Randall Havas has argued in *Nietzsche's Genealogy: Nihilism and the Will to Knowledge* that what Nietzsche means in his talk of the will to truth gaining self-consciousness is our becoming aware of its historical character (Havas, 1995: 163). He contends that the modern man of knowledge tends to deny that his commitment to truth is the product of religion, morality and philosophy since he holds that it constitutes a radical break with the past. By acknowledging its historical character, however, he affirms its necessity for him, and in doing so, he recognizes that it is of a piece with what he overcomes. In this way, Havas maintains, Nietzsche means 'to strengthen, not to weaken, our commitment to truthfulness' (Havas, 1995: xvii).

It is difficult to reconcile that reading with Nietzsche's claim that what distinguishes late modernity is the recognition that our commitment to truth depends on our need for error. Such recognition can surely not result in strengthening our commitment to truth. Indeed, not much sense can be made of the Nietzschean problematic of *the necessity of lies* on Havas's reading. Havas is right to insist that Nietzsche is not saying that our commitment to truth is to be overcome in favour of another one (Havas, 1995: 162). But that is because that commitment is to be put in the service of a different end than that of knowledge.

Tracy Strong's reading of what it means for the will to truth to gain self-consciousness in *Friedrich Nietzsche and the Politics of Transfiguration* is closer to the reading offered here. He says that this is the consciousness that there is no truth and that we should continue to seek it.

> Since Nietzsche has refused the succor of the realm of theoretical reason, the problems of truth must be found in practical reason. This latter, now detached from any possible link to a purer world, is a human responsibility: the contradictions are ours, and not just inherent in the relations between the theoretical and practical world. (Strong, 1988: 77)

As I see it, however, the question of truth for Nietzsche is addressed in the context of an ethics of self-constitution rather than in that of practical reason. Nietzsche's epistemology concludes with the thought that the categories of reason are fictions that have been employed in the formation of the human, all-too-human. It culminates in a consideration of the effects of truth on the self, of the way the narratives we tell ourselves about ourselves and the world have shaped us.[9]

Let me clarify this by considering what Nietzsche is doing in *On the Genealogy of Morals*. How are we to read his description of the slave revolt in morality in the First Essay, for example, or his account of the origin of the bad conscience in the Second Essay? Does Nietzsche claim to be describing historical facts or empirical origins?

And yet, how could they be taken in that way when Nietzsche asks his reader, in the final paragraphs of the *Genealogy*, to call the value of truth into question? Doesn't that question cast an uneasy light on everything he has been telling us about morality, the bad conscience and the ascetic ideal up to that point?

Strong puts his finger on how to approach that problem when he remarks the following:

> What Nietzsche comes to see in the course of his investigations is that illness he diagnosed – the development and triumph of nihilism in Western culture – goes far beyond a temporary aberration. It will not be possible to simply *tell* people what is wrong, for the very *manner in which they understand* the world will not permit them to understand the problem at hand.... No matter how good or complete the account of what has happened, unless a change in the manner of understanding is provoked, the account will remain merely a museum. (Strong, 1988: 31)

That rightly suggests that what Nietzsche tells us is not to be taken from a third person standpoint as a series of objective facts. But how is that change in our way of understanding to be accomplished? Through a kind of exercise, an exercise of the will to truth.

Nietzsche's discourse on slave morality (say) has no representational content or truth-value. It is more of the order of a biographical narrative that shapes our self-understanding than a statement about what is the case. The entire force of this discourse concentrates itself in the kind of obstacle it presents to our self-understanding. Its language, style and content are meant to bring about 'a new series of experiences' (Nietzsche, 1989: 261), that is, they are designed to create a context of meaning in which to interpret who we are, or better, how we have become who we are. Nietzsche remarks early on in *On the Uses and Disadvantages of History for Life*:

> A historiography could be imagined which had in it not a drop of common empirical truth and yet could lay claim to the highest degree of objectivity. (Nietzsche, 1997: 91)

A context of meaning like his discourse on slave morality might be called *objective* in the sense that it provides the reader with an anchor for making sense of her past and present behaviour without itself, however, being either true or false.

For Nietzsche, the narratives that constitute our self-understanding – the Platonic or Judeo-Christian accounts of man and the world – allow us to make sense of what we do and believe, but they don't represent facts (although they claim to). Strong remarks:

> Nietzsche ... thinks that societies dwell in the metaphors men take to be true since they have been so 'worn out' that they no longer appear as human creations. (Strong, 1988: 38)

There is no good reason to read Nietzsche's narratives on slave morality or on the origin of the bad conscience otherwise than as *metaphors* in that extended sense. The question we must ask in reading them is not *Is it true?* but *What if I were to accept it as true? What if I were to see my actions and beliefs as manifesting slave morality? What effect would that have on my self-understanding?* The question for Nietzsche is whether his reader has the strength to incorporate such contexts of meaning as he designs in the *Genealogy* and elsewhere and whether she is able to endure the light they shed on her actions and beliefs. That, I take it, is the experimentation with truth that he calls for in *Beyond Good and Evil*. What is at stake for Nietzsche is the kind of effects that our commitment to the truthfulness of certain narratives has on the self.[10]

Nietzsche's concern with that kind of exercise and discipline of the will is not limited to the will to truth. There is first his description in the Second Essay of the training and education that gives rise to the sovereign individual. The question here is how to breed an animal with the right to make promises (Nietzsche, 1989: 57).[11] That question is at the heart of Nietzsche's thought at the time, as two notes written in 1887 demonstrate. He says in the first one,

> I also want to make asceticism natural again: in place of the aim of denial, the aim of strengthening; a gymnastics of the will ... One should even devise tests for one's strength in being able to keep one's word. (Nietzsche, 1968: 483)

The second note says,

> What has been *spoiled* by the church's misuse of it:
>
> 1. *Ascesis*: one no longer really dares to point out the natural usefulness of ascesis, its indispensability in the service of *educating the will*. Our absurd world of educators ... believes it can make do with 'instruction', with dressage of the brain; it lacks even the concept that something else must come *first* – education of the *will-power*. Examinations are set in everything except the main issue: whether one is capable of *willing*, entitled to *promise*: the young man *finishes* his education without having so much as a question, a curiosity about this highest value problem of his nature.

In the Second Essay, Nietzsche describes the sovereign individual as a person who gives his word reluctantly and slowly, whose trust is 'a mark of *distinction*', since it is something that can be relied on. He knows himself 'strong enough to maintain it in the face of accidents'. His is a 'proud awareness of the extraordinary privilege of *responsibility*'. The 'consciousness of this rare freedom, this power over oneself and over fate, has in his case ... become instinct, the dominating instinct ... this sovereign individual calls it his *conscience*' (Nietzsche, 1989: 59–60).

Nietzsche has most likely in mind the famous story of the Roman consul Regulus, as Cicero tells it in *On Duties*. Captured by the Carthaginians in the First Punic War, Regulus was sent to the Senate after having sworn an oath that he would come back to Carthage unless certain noble captives were returned to the Carthaginians. He went to Rome and pleaded that the captors not be returned to the enemy. His authority prevailed. The captives were held back, and he returned to Carthage, knowing fully well that he was going to a cruel death. Cicero (1928: 43) tells us that in all this, Regulus thought that his oath should be kept.

Secondly, Nietzsche refers to Julius Caesar in *Twilight of the Idols* as the type of individual who defended himself against sickliness and headache with 'tremendous marches, the simplest form of living, uninterrupted sojourn in the open air, continuous toil'. One would have to find the highest type of free man, he continues in another note, where the greatest resistance is constantly being overcome:

> Five steps from tyranny, near the threshold of servitude. This is true psychologically when one understands by 'tyrants' pitiless and dreadful instincts, to combat which demands the maximum of authority and discipline toward oneself – finest type Julius Caesar. (Nietzsche, 1990: 96, 104)

These examples make clear that the goal of this practice of self-discipline is not *ataraxia*, a state of mental tranquility, as it is for the Stoics and Epicureans. It seeks peace neither in nor from this world. Displeasures are not avoided because they count as harmful or bad. Suffering is not denied and does not lead to self-denial. Displeasures and suffering are met as resistances that have to be made serviceable. They are sought out as incentives for gaining a greater measure of control over oneself and for training and exercising the will.[12]

In Nietzsche's eyes, the greatest and most difficult challenge that faces the modern human being is the extent to which he is able to remain well disposed towards himself with the insight into error as a necessary condition of conscious life. The assertion that truth is a kind of error can be seen as a challenge to the reader in Nietzsche's final texts. It is a challenge designed to initiate an exercise of the will. How will the reader encounter that proposition? She will no doubt encounter it at first as something that she will immediately and naturally refuse to believe, as a 'questionable' and 'dangerous' proposition that threatens her participation in daily life, as a resistance that must be overcome. Far from bringing the reader in harmony with becoming, that proposition is meant to force her to consider whether she has the strength to incorporate it as a habitual outlook on life, whether she can view life from the tragic standpoint where its meaningfulness depends on errors that she has accepted as true. To engage in that type of exercise would be to move in the direction of a critical ethos in which the history of truth would vanish into a final and lasting *epoché*.

8. *Schein*

Does that practice of self-discipline presuppose, as a necessary condition of possibility, the forgottenness of being?

No doubt, that practice takes place by suspending metaphysical characterizations of the world as being or as becoming, as reality or as appearance. But that suspension doesn't entail that it operates without some understanding of being. Put differently, as long as something *shows up* in that practice and is *intelligible* to it, there prevails an understanding of being.

How do things show up in that practice? They show up as appearances. We are asked to incorporate the insight that the propositions that we have hitherto accepted as true are based on errors. Such things are called *seemings*. They pretend to be real, or they seduce us into the belief that they are real when they are not. Such things are distinguished from realities.

What else should be understood by *appearance* in this context?

Heidegger reads Nietzsche's note on truth with which I began this chapter at the end of his 1936 lecture, *The Will to Power as Art*. Nietzsche says in the note:

> *Truth is the kind of error* without which a particular kind of living creature could not live. The value for life is what ultimately decides. (Nietzsche, 2003: 16)

Heidegger's interpretation of that note in that lecture is markedly different from his argument in *Plato's Doctrine of Truth* (1931/2) and *The Will to Power as Knowledge* (1939). The section in which Heidegger cites the note in *The Will to Power as Art* is titled *The New Interpretation of Sensuousness and the Raging Discordance between Art and Truth*. Heidegger's question is how the constitution of the sensuous should be understood in the context of Nietzsche's overturning of Platonism.

The overturning of Platonism involves the revaluation of the hierarchical structure that orders the supersensuous and the sensuous. For Plato, the supersensuous is the world of unchanging truths or Forms. The sensuous is the world of seemings. Since seemings are pale reflections, shadows or copies of truth, the sensuous is secondary or dependent on the supersensuous. The supersensuous renders it intelligible and brings it about. For Platonism, the supersensuous is of more value than the sensuous.

Heidegger focuses, throughout his lecture, on Nietzsche's phrase that art is worth more than truth. That phrase enacts *in nuce* the overturning of Platonism.

Once Platonism is overturned, the sensuous is no longer conceived as a copy of the supersensuous. The sensuous is what gives birth to the supersensuous. Citing Nietzsche's note above, Heidegger remarks that *truth* refers to a vanishing appearance that has been fixed and made constant. That is how the supersensuous arises.

Truth does not become a non-being in Nietzsche's overturning of Platonism. It is a kind of appearance that Heidegger qualifies as *mere appearance, bloßen Scheins*. It is a seeming that is necessary for life.

What makes possible appearance in general? There would be neither seemings nor realities, neither appearances nor truths, neither the sensuous nor the supersensuous unless something showed up and came to light. On Heidegger's reading, the perspectival for Nietzsche is what, in advance and before every ontic determination, makes possible light and appearing. The perspectival is appearing proper, the bringing-to-appearance of what there is.

> *aller Anschein und aller Scheinbarkeit nur möglich ist, wenn überhaupt sich etwas zeigt und zum Vorschein kommt. Was ein solches Erscheinen im voraus ermöglicht, ist das Perspektivische selbst. Dieses ist das eigentliche Scheinen, zum sich-zeigen-Bringen.* (N1 215)

Heidegger cites one of Nietzsche's notes in which he writes that *Schein* is 'the actual and sole reality of things'. That does not mean, Heidegger says, that reality is something merely apparent. It means that *to be* is to be *perspectival*. It is to *bring* something *to appearance, to let shine, to let it*, an entity, *shine in itself.*

> *das Realsein ist in sich perspektivisch, ist ein zum-Vorschein-Bringen, ein Scheinenlassen, in sich ein Scheinen; Realität ist Schein ... Die Realität, das Sein, ist der Schein im Sinne des perspektivischen Scheinenlassens.* (N1 215)

Being in Nietzsche means appearing in the sense of perspectival letting-appear.

The thrust of Heidegger's interpretation in this final section of the lecture is not merely that it presents Nietzsche as a proto-phenomenologist. Heidegger seems to be suggesting that Nietzsche's interpretation of the will to power as art recovers a sense of being, beyond its forgottenness, as light, appearing or disclosure.

Does this mean that Nietzsche's text recognizes, however obliquely, the alterity of being in relation to entities? *Schein* properly means light, radiance or appearance. That is presumably to be taken in the verbal sense as the articulation of the intelligibility of entities, as their coming-to-appearance, rather than in the nominal sense, as referring to a thing that appears.

Schein in that verbal sense vanishes, however, with truth understood as the drive to arrest and fix what flows and moves. Truth turns the movement of appearing into *a thing that endures* and *is constant*. *Truth* in Nietzsche, Heidegger says, means a true being (*wahrhaft Seiendes*). And that means, in turn, something constant and fixed (*Beständiges, Festgemachtes*) (N1 214).

Is it as *light* and *appearing* that the practice of self-discipline understands being? Perhaps. In the final analysis, however, one thing is certain. This is that *Heidegger's Nietzsche*, whatever else that figure may signify, is as protean as *Nietzsche*. That figure is not reducible to *the last great metaphysician of the West*. She also thinks from the finitude of philosophy.

Substance

To produce a good metaphor is to see a likeness.

—Aristotle, *Poetics*

The metaphorical exists only within metaphysics.
—Martin Heidegger, *The Principle of Reason*

1. Introduction

In this chapter, I argue that the appearance of *substantia* as a technical term in the language of the Romans between the first century BC and the fourth century AD testifies to an understanding of being that is distinct from the one in Classical Greece and in early Christian thought, and that what makes possible the appearance of *substantia* in that sense is the play of a pair of metaphors.

In the next section, I review the standard hypothesis on the genesis of the concept of substance in Roman thought. In section 3, I briefly examine the emergence of the concept of *essentia* in early Christian thought. In section 4, I turn to Seneca and Cicero in order to show that it is in the context of the use of the metaphorical pair *solidity/likeness* that *substantia* enters the written discourse of the Romans as a philosophical term.

In section 5, I describe the context of experience that governs the use of that metaphorical pair. In section 6, I consider what should be understood by the expression *metaphor* in this instance. That provides me with the opportunity to return to an issue that was left inexplicit in Chapter 3. That is the meaning of the use of the word *figure* in the expression *figuration of being*.

2. The standard hypothesis

Few concepts have enjoyed a greater destiny in Western philosophical discourse than that of *substance*. Proclaimed by some as the most pregnant of terms for metaphysics and physics (Leibniz), decried by others as the emptiest of terms (Locke), the concept of substance has functioned throughout modern times as a pole of attraction and hostility, of inspiration and criticism.

No doubt, it is no longer charged today with the exorbitant value it once possessed during the period between Descartes and Hegel. Even so, its central importance for the early moderns and for the scholastics suffices to make us wonder about its first appearance in philosophical discourse.

Moreover, the term is the cause of some difficulty in the secondary literature on Aristotle. Commentators are well aware of the fact that *substance* is not a satisfying term for rendering the Greek *ousia*, even as they follow their medieval predecessors in using it for making sense of that term in Aristotle.[1] It is rarely asked why *substance* is a misleading term for *ousia*. It is even more rarely asked what that term originally meant, in what kind of contexts it arose and was first used, and what matters pressing to human concern it was meant to address and articulate.

This chapter intends to broach these questions. I argue that the appearance of the notion of substance as a technical term in the discourse of the Romans in the period between the first century BC and the fourth century AD bears witness to an understanding of being that is markedly distinct from that of the Classical Greeks and from that of early Christian thought.

The OED confirms the analyses conducted by some of the authors on the topic.[2] It is said that the first known use of *substantia* in Seneca translates a Greek term, although it has not always been clear what that term is.

Curt Arpe (1941: 67, 65) proposed long ago that *substantia* translates the Stoic *upostasis*. That term, he tells us, signifies 'actual, corporeal being', 'reality'. René Braun (1977: 172) suggests that Seneca often uses *substantia* to render the Stoic verb *uphestekenai*. That term has the same meaning as the former, but with a more emphatic accent on the idea of 'a substrate persisting as the basis and ground of particular things'.

A brief glance at the non-philosophical use of *substantia* that appears in works written in the post-Republican period shows that such claims are not accurate. The standard hypothesis is that *substantia* is the product of a technical invention and that it was invented to translate a Greek term from which it derives its meaning. The evidence, however, suggests the contrary.

Forged from the verb *substare*, the construction of *substantia* probably followed the same pattern as *constantia, distantia, instantia, circumstantia* – terms composed with the suffix *-antia* from *stare*, which means *stability, firmness, immovable presence*. *Substantia* is found in diverse authors without any philosophical or technical sense from AD 50 onwards.

In Frontinus's (1925: I.26) *De Aquis*, for instance, the term signifies 'the basis of an evaluation'. Tacitus (2001: 8.3) stresses its etymological value in *Dialogus de oratoribus*, 'that which supports'. And Quintilian (1924: VI, *prooem.* 7) uses it sometimes to designate 'wealth'.

Or take as witness the juridical language that constitutes itself around the first and second centuries AD where the semantic range of the term includes 'goods', 'patrimony', 'matter' and 'content' (see Gaius, 1988: II.79 and Pseudo-Quintilian, 1982: XIV).

Substantia is from the start a semantically rich and flexible notion. It is unlikely that its meaning derives solely from the Greek *upostasis*. That is doubly confirmed by the appearance of the term in the Antehieronymian translations of the Bible, in the oldest versions of the New Testament. Joseph de Ghellinck (1941: 88–95) has shown that *substantia* renders *upostasis* as well as *ta uparchonta, ta schemata, ousia* and even *bios*. Since all of these Greek terms resonate with *substantia*, its meaning cannot have been derived from one of them.

It is only with Boethius that, driven by the need to establish correspondences in Latin with Greek theological notions, *substantia* is reduced to a univocal sense. In *Contra Eutychen*, a letter on the theological controversy on the double nature of Christ, human and divine, Boethius (1997: III.42–101) fixes the equation *substantia* = *upostasis*, which will remain in force throughout the Middle Ages.

The ordinary senses of *substantia*, its semantic wealth, and the derivatives constructed from the same root all point to its having an indigenous character. It is likely that it was used in oral discourse prior to Seneca. It is possible, too, that the entry of *substantia* in the written language of the Romans is prompted by its encounter with Greek thought and language. But it is evident from its first philosophical use in Seneca that the term has a distinct Latin ring.

Courtine (2003: 59) argues in *Les catégories de l'être* that the philosophical use of *substantia* from Seneca to Boethius is semantically uniform. He writes:

> It is as if the word *substantia* … had for aim the thematic development of an immediate understanding of being as corporeality, solidity, ground.

Courtine is right that, in the period between Seneca and Boethius, *substantia* expresses the idea that *to be* is to be *corporeal* (although the development of that understanding is doubtless less thematic, that is, less conscious or reflective, than he seems to suggest). The analyses that he conducts, however, do not tell us how *substantia* becomes an ontological term. On what ground does the meaning of *substantia* as body express what counts as a being in contrast with a non-being? More generally, what makes it possible for being to say itself in a particular historical language?

As I argue in section 5, one of the constitutive elements of the factical life of the Romans is the enduring presence of conflicts between agents in the forum, in public assemblies, at law courts and in the senate. The experience of that *agon* in their daily life necessitated a reflection on the practice of politics, rhetoric and the judiciary. It produced a multiplicity of discourses on how to speak about what is just and unjust, good and bad, right and wrong. In that discursive field, we can detect a nascent articulation of the difference between being and non-being through a play of metaphors. It is within that context that *substantia* first emerges as an ontological term.

No doubt, the significance of Epicureanism and, above all, of Stoicism in the language and thought of the Romans cannot be underestimated. But its importance for the appearance of the ontological use of *substantia* in Rome should also not be overestimated.

Greek thought from Parmenides to the Stoics takes root in an entirely different kind of problematic than that in which Roman thought forges its vocabulary of being. Nothing animated Greek thought so much as the question *What is nature?* It involved, among other things, the question of motion or becoming, its principles, whether they are one or many, the paradoxes of becoming, the question of whether a science or discourse of becoming is possible, and so on. Greek thinking is a thinking of *phusis* in the manifold senses of that term (origin, principle, essence, cause, nature, being, movement, world, etc.).

Roman thought awakens before an entirely different kind of problematic. It is not the perplexities experienced before *phusis* that initiates Roman thinking. Accordingly, an examination of Epicurean or Stoic notions will tell us little about the horizon to which the ontological use of *substantia* immediately responds.

Heidegger writes in *The Origin of the Work of Art* that Roman–Latin thought takes over Greek words without a corresponding, equally genuine experience of what they say (*PLT* 23). My aim in what follows is to demarcate the horizon of experience in which *substantia* appears as an ontological term in the writings of the Romans.

Or again, Cicero says in *De finibus* (1994: III.I.3–4) that we have to create a vocabulary, invent new words, to convey new things. The question is what 'new things' the Romans had to convey when they introduced *substantia* as a central word in their vocabulary of being.

3. Essence

Seneca's *Letter* 58 is particularly interesting in that regard. In his preamble on the poverty of the Latin language, Seneca (1925: 58.6) introduces *essentia* as a translation for *ousia*. He says that this Greek term designates the nature that contains the foundation of all things. But in the course of his discussion, he uses *substantia* instead. Why?

Essentia is a word formed from *ens* (a being), the present participle of the infinitive *esse* (to be). That link was probably modelled on the derivation of *ousia* from *ousa*, the feminine present participle of the infinitive *einai* (to be). A word designed strictly to match the construction of a Greek term, *essentia* has no colloquial resonances when it first appears in written discourse. Hesitant about that term, Seneca (1925: 58.6) hopes to obtain a 'favourable hearing' about it from Lucilius. Quintilian regards it as 'unduly harsh'. Conscious of the fact that *essentia* is the correct translation of *ousia*, Apuleius (1997: I.VI, 326–8) nevertheless uses *substantia* in his discourse on Plato.

Essentia remains a floating signifier up until the time of the Gallo-Roman poet Sidonius Apollinaris (AD 430–89). He uses it at *Carmen* XV.102–17 in his Neoplatonic account of the generation of the world but reverts back to the more customary use of *substantia* in the rest of his poem.

The establishment of *essentia* as a central ontological term takes place in the fifth century AD in a theological context. Under pressure to specify, against their Greek counterparts, the idea that God is one *ousia* and three *upostaseis*, Latin theologians use *essentia* for God and *substantia* for the Three Persons.[3] In Boethius, Augustine and others, *essentia* designates the incorporeal activity of the divine cause. Pierre Hadot (1968: 490–3) has shown that this understanding of *essentia*, and thus of being (*esse*) in Augustine and Boethius, is the direct result of the Porphyrian–Neoplatonic understanding of being (*einai*) as the incorporeal cause of corporeal things.

On the other hand, what the Romans of the period that we are studying immediately hear in the word *ousia* is the semantic content that vibrates first and foremost in some of the colloquial resonances of *substantia*: body, solidity, matter. Such different authors as Cicero, Lucan, Tertullian and Calcidius bear witness to that mundane understanding of being, as does Seneca in *Letter* 58.[4]

4. Substance

Seneca introduces *essentia* in *Letter* 58 to render the Platonic notion of *ousia*. He tells Lucilius that he wants to examine the different meanings of Plato's expression for 'being' (*to on*). Before doing so, he opens two parentheses. In the first parenthesis (1925: 58.8–14), he gives an exposition of Aristotle's method of division, the classification of universals into genera and species. In the second parenthesis (15), he turns to the Stoic doctrine of the supreme genus, the something (*ti*) beyond being.

No doubt, Seneca's interpretation of Aristotle's method is heterodox. He says that being is the supreme genus because there is no term superior to it.

> It is the beginning of all things (*initium rerum est*); and all things fall under it (*omnia sub illo sunt*). (12)

Seneca is probably relying on a confused Middle Platonist manual since neither Plato nor Aristotle speaks of being as a supreme genus.[5] He illustrates the Aristotelian method of division by proceeding first from the indivisible species to the highest genus and then by moving back in reverse order. In both cases, he divides being into the corporeal and the incorporeal (11, 14).[6]

The second parenthesis opens with the claim that the Stoics set above being another, even higher genus. There is a genus beyond being which they call *quid = ti, something*. And he explains their reasoning,

> In the order of nature some things exist (*quadam sunt*) and other things do not exist (*quae non sunt*). And even the things that do not exist are really part of the order of nature. What these are will readily occur to the mind, for example centaurs, giants, and all other figments of unsound reasoning (*falsa cogitatione*), which have begun to have a definite shape (*habere aliquam imaginem*), although *non habeat substantiam*. (15)

The translator of Seneca's *Epistles* renders the last expression as follows: 'although they have no bodily consistency' (15).

Beings and non-beings for the Stoics fall under the genus *something*. Non-beings like centaurs or giants are not nothing. They are *something* because they are conceived by the mind: they are its intentional objects. Now when Seneca refers to non-beings in this passage, to the sort of things that have no *ousia*, we would expect him to say, *non habeat essentiam*, 'they have no essence'. Instead, he says, *non habeat substantiam*. Why this sudden shift in terminology when a few paragraphs earlier he had stressed that *essentia* is the correct word for *ousia*?

Presumably, that has to do with the fact that *substantia* allows him to say something in this context that the usage of *essentia* would not have readily conveyed to his reader, namely, that things like centaurs and giants, which have no bodily existence, have also no being. This means that *substantia* signifies at once and irreducibly both being (*esse*) and body (*corpus*), and *a fortiori* being *as* body.[7]

That passage is interesting in another respect as well. It uses the opposition between having substance (*habere substantiam*) and having the likeness of one (*habere imaginem*). *Imaginem* is the accusative case of *imago*. In Seneca's language, it is associated with *similitudo*. It means *image, likeness, seeming* or *appearance*. That opposition is Stoic in appearance.[8] In truth, however, it is adapted to cover the much more specifically Roman contrast between solidity and likeness (*res/similitudo, solidum/imago*). The latter is found in a number of different contexts in both Cicero and Seneca.

There is, first of all, Seneca's *De vita beata*. Following the Greek dogma that the happy life is the good life, Seneca asks whether pleasure or virtue – the Epicurean or Stoic end – constitutes the good life.

> Let us seek something that is a good more than in appearance (*non in speciem bonum*) – something that is constant (*sed solidum*) and more beautiful in its more hidden part. (Seneca, 1935: III.1)

He deploys a number of arguments in this essay to prove that pleasure is inconstant. He notes at one point that pleasure subsides at the moment when it is most enjoyed. The desire for pleasure is instantaneously gratified and its recurrence is incessantly demanded. It comes and goes like the rhythm of a Heraclitean flux.

> Nor is anything certain (*certum*) whose nature consists in movement. So it is not even possible that there should be any *substantia* in that which comes and goes most swiftly and will perish in the very exercise of its power. (Seneca, 1935: VII. 4)

Pleasure has no substance because it is inconstant. It provides no certainty and firmness (*inconstantiam*: VIII. 6). Virtue has substance because it is constant, solid, stable. Pleasure enslaves because it places us at the mercy of fortune, of whatever comes to gratify the body. Virtue liberates because it is concerned with the harmony of the soul and with its tranquillity. It furnishes an immovable foundation (*fundamentum grave, immobile*: XV.4) in life because it frees the soul from the hazards of chance and draws it back to reason and to the rationality of the universe.

There is, in the second place, Cicero's use of this opposition in at least three different texts:

i. Cicero (2001: III.I.3) criticises the best of the Romans for following public opinion at the start of Book III of *Tusculan Disputations*. They strain to win not the superior image of virtue but a shadowy phantom of glory (*imaginem gloriae*) when true glory (*gloria solida*) is a thing of real worth (*res*) and clearly wrought, no shadowy phantom.

ii. He criticizes Epicurus's doctrine of the formation of the notion of god in
     De natura deorum. He tells us that according to Epicurus, we envisage
     god's appearance by thought rather than with the senses. His form has no
     solidity (*soliditatem*), and our perception of it is such that it is discerned in
     a sequence of similar images (*similitudine*). These images emerge from a
     limitless number of atoms acting on our thought and, as a result, our minds
     see the divine nature as blessed and eternal. Cicero (1935: I.105) wonders:

> 'If the gods make their impact only on our thoughts and have no
> solidity (*soliditatem*) ... what difference does it make whether we visualize
> a hippocentaur or a god?'

Cicero's reference to the centaur is interesting. It is regularly cited as
an example of what does not exist, as in Seneca's *Letter* 58. It means that
the opposition between *solidum* and *similitudo*, which governs here the
contrast between what is known through the senses and what is known
through thought, is immediately ontological. Anything that is sensible is
solid. It is certain and reliable. It *exists* in the genuine and proper sense
of the term. It cannot be other than how it shows itself to the eyes or the
touch. It manifests itself just as it is without delay.

It is otherwise with images and other phantoms of the brain. Epicurus
claims that we have images of the gods as living a blessed and eternal life
and that those images result from the action of their atoms on our mind.
But those atoms are insensible. Accordingly, we cannot be certain that what
acts on our thought are the atoms of the gods rather than of centaurs. What
is insensible has a shadowy existence, a being in appearance only. It can be
other than how it shows itself through the images it produces on our mind.

iii. Cicero (2003: 27) distinguishes between two kinds of definition in the *Topica*
     on the basis of the ontological content of that contrast. There are definitions
     of things that exist, and there are definitions of things that are thought:

> The things which I say exist (*esse*) are those which can be seen and
> touched, like a piece of land, a house, a wall, a gutter, a slave, food and so
> on ... Those things I say have no being (*non esse*) which cannot be touched
> and pointed out but which nevertheless can be understood and grasped
> by the soul, for example, if you define acquiring ownership, guardianship,
> family, agnation; these things have no underlying body (*subest ... corpus*),
> as it were, but a pattern and a concept stamped and imprinted on the mind
> which I call a notion.

It is likely that this type of expression – *habens subesse corpus* – played an important role in the emergence of the concept of *substantia* in philosophical circles, as Courtine (2003: 58) and Braun (1977) remark. Seneca's expression in *Letter 58*, *habere substantiam*, testifies to that.

But the opposition between *solidum* and *imago* also played a significant role in that regard. Tobias Reinhardt (in Cicero, 2003: 259) suggests that Cicero's three-tiered distinction in this passage has its origin not in any particular philosophical school – whether in the Epicurean, Stoic or Platonic school – but in Roman rhetoric and legal thought itself. There is, firstly, the distinction between being and non-being. Corresponding to this, there is the distinction between the corporeal and the incorporeal. Lastly and correspondingly, there is the distinction between two types of definition. As I have shown, the first of these two distinctions is governed by the play of a pair of metaphors, *solidum/ imago*.

Seneca uses this pair in the peroration of *Letter 58*, which specifies his use of the distinction between 'having substance' and 'having the likeness of one' in the passage cited above. He wonders how Plato's theory of Forms contributes to our moral improvement. What can we draw from them that will put a check on our appetites?

> Perhaps the very thought, that all these things which minister to our senses, which arouse and excite us, are by Plato denied a place among the things that truly exist (*esse quae vere sint*). Such things are therefore likenesses (*imaginaria*), and though they for the moment present a certain external appearance, yet they are in no case stable or solid (*stabile nec solidum est*). (Seneca, 1925: 58.26–7)

That passage is interesting. It shows that the pair *solidum/imago* can be employed to express the ontological pre-eminence of the incorporeal over the corporeal, as it is here, or, conversely, of the corporeal over the incorporeal, as in the earlier passage on the Stoic doctrine of the supreme genus and in Cicero. What that pair achieves, in both cases, is an articulation of the difference between being and non-being. It is the linguistic node that makes possible the Roman understanding of being.

Substantia becomes an ontological term not because it translates the Greek or Stoic *upostasis*, but on condition that it enters the play of that turn of phrase, *that's solid, it's solid in appearance only*.

The question now is what the context of experience is that gives meaning to the Roman understanding of being as matter, body, solidity. That context of experience, I argue, is the Roman reflection on the practice of rhetoric.

5. Rhetoric

It is well known that rhetoric establishes itself as first philosophy in Rome during the late Republican and early Imperial period.[9] That is evident from the fact that the hierarchy among the various disciplines and sciences is determined from the standpoint of rhetoric, which is concerned with the political sphere, rather than from that of the knowledge of first principles and causes, as in Aristotle. Philosophical problems generally (physical, ethical, theological) now fall within the purview of rhetoric, and philosophy itself is made subordinate to its cares and concerns.[10] Cicero (1960, 15.56–19.73) famously reclaims the ancient title of 'wisdom' for rhetoric in Book III of *De oratore* prior to its Socratic–Platonic division into philosophy and oratory.[11]

Renato Barilli (1989: 26) insists that this notion of rhetoric is not a peculiarity of Cicero's. It belongs to the entire way of life of the Roman Republic. That way of life is marked by the continuous presence of conflicts in the public sphere, which at times even extended beyond the grave.[12]

The matter brought before the orator is a conflict, whether in a lawsuit (*controversia*) or in a political debate (*contentio*). The function of rhetoric is to spell out the different types of questions that may arise in a conflict. The aim of rhetoric is not to resolve them. It is to equip the orator with strategies and lines of approach so that he can defeat his opponent and win glory and fame.

Plato's condemnation of rhetoric in the *Gorgias* (it's a knack used to gratify the soul with pleasure: 462C) and the *Phaedrus* (it has no method with which to arrive at the truth: 269D) had no influence on the Romans. It was otherwise with Aristotle's *Rhetoric*.

Rhetoric for Aristotle shares the same discursive space as philosophy (or dialectic). Neither of them is concerned with the true and the false but with the apparent and the probable, *phainomena* and *doxa* (Aristotle, 2000: 1404a1). That is because both rhetoric and dialectic have to do with matters that are within the cognizance of all humans and are not confined to any special science. Rhetoric has a non-specialized field, and its universality is co-extensive with that of dialectic (354a1–4).

Quintilian (1924) agrees with Aristotle in his *Institutiones oratoriae*. He remains faithful to the Aristotelian tradition in distinguishing between three kinds of discourse – deliberative, forensic and epideictic – in relation to the audience they address and the end the speaker has in view. One of the elements he adds to this tradition is Hermagoras's stasis theory, which is significant for my purpose.

By stasis, Hermagoras has in mind a discursive tool the orator uses to make sense of a conflict. A dispute is made intelligible when it is reduced to a series of precise questions so that what is at stake in it can be clearly identified. That is what the orator must focus on in building his attack or defence.[13] So, for example, when a dispute arises between the prosecutor's charge (*You did it*) and the defendant's counter-charge (*No, I did not do it*), the audience or jury will have to decide whether he did it and what he did. The orator will attend to these questions in constructing his discourse in order to persuade the audience or jury one way or the other.

Hermagoras calls his first stasis or question – *Did he do it?* – conjectural. The facts about the case have to be established or inferred by conjecture before anything else. The second question – *What did he do?* – is definitional, since once the facts about the case have been established their nature may still be in doubt.

He adds two further questions, one concerned with the quality of the action (e.g. *Was it right for the defendant to do this?*) and another about the competence of the tribunal to deal with the case at hand. Quintilian reduces this fourfold division of questions to an opposition between two terms, opposing the first question to the last three. The conjectural question is the primary one on which the understanding of the whole case depends. Since this question aims to establish the certain facts of the case, that will determine how the nature and quality of the facts are understood.[14] The last three questions are from this standpoint circumstantial.

> There is also another method of dividing the *status* into two classes: according to this, disputes are either about substance (*de substantia*) or quality (*de qualitate*). Substance is dealt with by conjecture; for in enquiring into anything, we ask whether it has been done, is being done, or is likely to be done. (Quintilian, 1924: III.6.39)

He reformulates this opposition once more, drawing this time on Theodorus of Gadara. According to Theodorus, there are two basic facts in a dispute that must be identified. The first is addressed by the question *peri ousias*, the second by the question *peri sumbebekoton*. Theodorus 'holds that the question is either as to whether such and such a thing is so (*an sit*), or is concerned with the accidents of something (*de accidentibus*) which is an admitted fact: that is to say it is either *peri ousias* or *peri sumbebekoton*' (Quintilian, 1924: III.6.36). Quintilian introduces in this context Aristotle's categories of being:

> Aristotle lays down that there are ten categories on which every question seems to turn. First there is *ousia*, which Plautus calls *essence*, the only available

translation: under this category we inquire *whether a thing is* (*an sit*). Secondly, there is *quality*, the meaning of which is self-evident. Third comes *quantity*. (III.6.23)

Courtine (2003: 47) rightly remarks that Quintilian may well recall the strict translation of *ousia* by *essentia*. But his interpretation of the question, *peri ousias* as the orator's line of approach for establishing the certain and solid facts of a dispute, inevitably leads him to reinstate the expression *substantia*.

Aristotle's categories of being find their way into rhetoric with Quintilian in the context of Hermagoras's stasis theory as discursive tools that furnish the orator with angles of attack and defence in a legal or political dispute. That will prove to be decisive for the nominalistic reception of Aristotle's *Categories* in Boethius and others.[15] Equally decisive for the history of commentaries on Aristotle from the fifth century AD to the present is the opposition between *substantia* and *accidens*, which appears here for the first time.

6. Metaphor

I have shown that the metaphorical pair *solidum/imago* articulates the difference between being and non-being in the factical life of the Romans. What is the connection between being and metaphor?

That connection was indirectly addressed in Chapter 3.2 where I argued that being is unthinkable except as a figuration of something or someone, that is, as a figure in which the force of the distinction between the *who* and the *what* is suspended. That a figure of speech or metaphor should articulate the difference between being and non-being, or that a figure like the feminine should make being thinkable, suggests that something other must be meant by *figure* or *metaphor* than what is ordinarily meant by these terms.

Heidegger briefly analyses the concept of metaphor on at least two occasions, first in his *Der Ister* lecture and then in Lecture 6 of *The Principle of Reason* (1955–6). On both of these occasions, he shows that metaphor is a metaphysical concept. In any given circumstance where a metaphor is used, the distinction between the sensuous and the non-sensuous is presupposed.

> The idea of 'transposing' and of metaphor is based upon the distinguishing, if not complete separation, of the sensible and the nonsensible as two realms that subsist on their own. The setting up of this partition between the sensible and the nonsensible, between the physical and nonphysical is a basic trait of what is called metaphysics and which normatively determines Western thinking. (*PR* 48)

The *sensuous* is not something in nature. Something is sensuous insofar as it is the image of something else. The sensuous is an appearance. It is an image that points away from itself to something other.

According to the metaphysical interpretation of art, that is the mode of being of the physical in the work. The river in Hölderlin's *Der Rhein*, for instance, is distinguished from the geographical river that goes by that name. Abstracted from nature, the river in the poem is usually seen as an image that conveys a non-sensuous idea or meaning. The *sensuous* is an image that points away from itself to something non-sensuous.

Accordingly, a metaphor, figure of speech or, generally speaking, a written or spoken symbol – that is, anything that is of the order of the image – is standardly conceived as the becoming-sensible of the non-sensible, as the temporalization or spatialization of a meaning or ideal object (see Derrida, 1982: 227–8). It is the work and product of the imagination, which shares in the sensuous and in the non-sensuous.

However, the pair *solidum/imago* is not a metaphor in that sense. These terms cannot be interpreted as a pair of images that make sensuous a non-sensuous meaning or content. Far from presupposing the distinction between the sensuous and the non-sensuous, the corporeal and the incorporeal, that turn of phrase first articulates and renders it intelligible in Roman thought.

Following Nietzsche's essay *On Truth and Lies in a Nonmoral Sense*, Derrida argues in *White Mythology* that an entire metaphorical language precedes and conditions the philosophical distinction and classification between idea and word, sensible and nonsensible, the literal and the figurative expression (such as the metaphor), and that that language cannot, therefore, still to be called *metaphorical*.

> But … can these defining tropes that are prior to all philosophical rhetoric and that produce philosophemes still be called metaphors? (Derrida, 1982: 255)

The same question might be posed about the pair *solidum/imago*, a turn of phrase whose textual use articulates how entities show up, that is, *as* sensuous or *as* nonsensuous. Either that turn of phrase cannot be identified with a metaphorical turn of phrase or, providing we insist on thinking of it as a figurative expression, the 'figurative' must be thought beyond the opposition between the sensuous and the non-sensuous, that is, beyond metaphysics.

Aristotle says in the *Poetics* that to produce a good metaphor we must observe a likeness between things. In *On Truth and Lies in a Nonmoral Sense*, Nietzsche says that a good metaphor (or concept) creates that likeness between things. It posits as equal or similar the unequal or dissimilar (*Gleichsetzen des Ungleichen*).

What we have in the case at hand is a figure of what is singular in the extreme, unlike anything else in the world, without precedent in nature or history. Perhaps such a figure should in truth be called a *non-figure*. Is the image of that which lacks a determinable identity as an entity (and, hence, as an image) still *an image*? I am not sure.

At any rate, the pair *solidum/imago* institutes the relation to being in the idiomatic language of the Romans. It makes possible the relation between Roman Dasein and entities in general. Far from being an accessory to or ornament of thought, this turn of phrase makes it possible to forget being.

Are we then better served to think of 'metaphor' as a condition necessary for being (the light in which entities show up) to have a history? How is this connection to be understood between the turn of phrase and the turn in or of being, the turn between forgetting and remembering, throwness and projection, need and belonging?

These are questions for another time, and another study.

Notes

Chapter 1

1   An early version of this chapter appeared in *Research in Phenomenology* Vol. 46
    (3) (2016) under the title 'Time, Singularity, and the Impossible: Heidegger and
    Derrida on Dying'.

2   On the extent of Heidegger's commitment to transcendental phenomenology, see
    Crowell's (2001: 167–81) reading of Heidegger and Husserl's failed collaboration
    on the *Encyclopaedia Britannica* article. Crowell rightly notes that Heidegger does
    not abandon the reduction (or some version of it) and that what signals his break
    with Husserl is his proposal for an ontology of the transcendental subject. That is
    something that, in Husserl's eyes, is inconceivable, since there are ontologies only
    of worldly entities and the transcendental subject is not a worldly entity. Crowell
    does not consider where Heidegger's proposal comes from. That is the strain of
    hermeneutics in his thinking. It is there from his first lecture in Freiburg onward.
    That puts him at odds with Husserl's transcendental phenomenology on a number of
    related issues as well, most significantly, perhaps, with the ideal of apodictic evidence,
    but also with transcendental reflection and description versus understanding and
    interpretation. See *TDP*, 85 where Heidegger agrees with Natorp's criticism of
    Husserl, that description, being conceptual, modifies the experience that is being
    described, and *TDP*, 98 where Heidegger proposes instead a 'hermeneutical intuition'
    of life. On the early Heidegger, see Van Buren (1994) and Kisiel (1995).

3   Drawing on the phenomenologies of Heidegger and Merleau-Ponty, Hubert Dreyfus
    (1972) argues in his first book that intelligence presupposes embodiment and
    embeddedness in a social context and that machines can't think because they are
    neither embodied nor embedded. Heidegger, it seems, would disagree. A sufficient
    condition for human intelligence or understanding, in my view, is historical and/
    or narrative self-awareness (consciousness of one's continuity through time, of
    one's beginning, middle and end). I cannot think of any good reason for ruling out,
    from the realm of the conceivable, that a machine could have such an awareness
    or, said differently, that the most a machine could conceivably exhibit is an
    instantaneous mind.

4   Derrida has pointed out in numerous essays the theoretical and ethical problems
    relating to Heidegger's generic use of the word 'animal'. See, for instance, Derrida
    (2008). Hence my use of scare quotes around the term.

5 Derrida (2001: 58): 'the most tempting figure for this absolute secret is death'.

6 We might think of the relation to death as the antithesis of the transcendental object in Kant. The latter is the unity of the concept of the object that makes possible the unity of the subject, or self-identity.

7 That poses a problem for my interpretation of the sentence *Ableben aber kann des Dasein nur solange, als er sterbt* in section 2.

8 Levinas's interpretation of Heidegger's being-toward-death in *Time and the Other* is doubtless in the background of Blanchot's reading here. But Blanchot seems to me to be much closer to the spirit of Heidegger, particularly to the thinking of the ontico-ontological difference – which is what is at stake here – than Levinas.

9 Levinas (1987: 71–2) says in *Time and the Other* that the Epicurean adage 'insists on the eternal futurity of death. The fact that it deserts every present [is due] to the fact that death is *ungraspable*'. As I see it, Heidegger and Levinas share the same notion of death, but they draw opposite conclusions from it. Notably, Levinas thinks that it puts an end to the subject's 'virility' and 'heroism' and introduces an extreme passivity and a relation to the other human being, whereas Heidegger thinks, at least in *Being and Time*, that it makes possible an authentic self-appropriation. Even if the latter were possible, which I'm not convinced of, I do not see why it would have to be either virile or heroic. See Chapter 2.

10 See also Derrida's (1991: 100, 107) remarks on Dasein in '"Eating Well," or the Calculation of the Subject: An Interview with Jacques Derrida.'

11 Two numerically distinct individuals, Plato and Socrates, are materially different but formally the same, since they share the form of *humanity*. Numerical distinctness presupposes sameness of concept or form. Uniqueness does not.

12 *To disclose* is to project meaning, a horizon of possibility, or world. *To be disclosed* is to find oneself in a meaningful situation with others, things and oneself.

13 Perhaps the problem is that transcendental phenomenology knows no limits. Eugen Fink (1995: 61–2), for instance, remains on the fence when he considers the question whether the transcendental constituting life has a beginning and end in birth and death.

14 Derrida seems to be modelling the structure of mourning on the structure of the subject's encounter with the other in Levinas. Levinas claims that the other who stands before me in a conversation transcends the idea I have of him, which reveals his alterity or uniqueness.

15 Some of the language is reminiscent of *What is Metaphysics?*: 'In the clear night of the nothing'. (*BW* 103).

Chapter 2

1 David Wood (2005: 65) contends that Levinas's argument is too weak to produce that desired conclusion. All that the relation with the alterity of death shows is

that the self is in relation with something with which it has nothing in common. It leaves 'indeterminate as to whether [this something] refers to a god, a rock, a cloud, nothingness'. I think that Wood is right. Why should *absolute alterity* mean the alterity of the other human being rather than, say, the alterity of being in relation to beings, which is what it signifies for Heidegger (see Chapter 3.2)? The translator of *Time and the Other*, Richard Cohen, inserts a footnote at this point of the argument on p. 75, presumably to reassure the reader that the text is not prey to 'an intellectual confusion or a fallaciously employed ambiguity', clearly sensing that something is awry here. Levinas is on more solid ground, I think, in *Totality and Infinity*, where he turns the encounter with the alterity of my death into a modality of the encounter with the other human being, instead of making the encounter with the other human being a modality of the alterity of my death. See Levinas, 1979: 234.

2   Levinas does not distinguish between the self and the ego in this text, that is, between the accusative *me* that is there at the pre-reflexive level of awareness, and the nominative *I*, the product of self-consciousness and self-identification, as he will do in later works.

3   The evocation of the *dialectic* as the method used in the text is perhaps not incidental. See Levinas (1987: 92).

4   On formalization versus generalization, see *PRL* 39–46.

Chapter 3

1   Bernasconi (2005: 172): 'My claim is that without addressing Darwin directly, Levinas uses Heidegger's ontology as a surrogate for Darwinism, social Darwinism and related ideas. By doing so, he finds a way of confronting the idea of a struggle for existence in terms of his own choosing.'

2   I sympathize with David Wood's (2005: 54) suggestion that it would be better to take Levinas's misreadings of Heidegger as a point of departure for a reflection on what is involved in reading another philosopher and on the ethical dimensions of that relationship. I wonder whether one of the reasons for Levinas's mischaracterizations of Heidegger's position, other than the fact that Heidegger joined the NSDAP in 1933, might be what Harold Bloom called *anxiety of influence*.

3   Many more could be cited. For instance: Jean Greisch (2005) in *Ethics and Ontology: some Hypocritical Reflections*, Rudi Visker (2004) in *The Inhuman Condition*, or Françoise Dastur (2002) in *The Call of Conscience: The Most Intimate Alterity*.

4   That means that the notion of *theory* or of *the theoretical* that becomes predominant in philosophy after Plato and Aristotle is understood as a suspension of work, that is, always by reference to work and production.

5   Levinas (1979: 46) also identifies ontology with a philosophy of power on the ground that, given the primacy of the theoretical attitude, the relation with the other human being consists in comprehending him, in grasping him under the identity of an impersonal concept. The violence of that impersonality, for Levinas, is concretely realized in the state.

6   See *MFL* 219 for Heidegger's interpretation of Plato's expression in *The Republic* and Levinas, 1979: 102–4.

7   That statement is the antithesis of Nicholas of Cusa's (1973: 31) definition of God, which is thought on the basis of identity pure and simple: 'the "not-other" is not other than the not-other'.

8   No doubt that dis-identification of the feminine with empirical beings of the female sex or gender doesn't temper the manifest androcentrism of Levinas's text, as Chanter (2005: 319) rightly observes. I think that Diane Perpich (2001: 36) is right when she remarks that, in *Totality and Infinity*, Levinas relegates the feminine being 'to those domains that have traditionally been both her purview and her lot: on the one hand, the home and domestic arrangements, and on the other, the erotic relationship and maternity', even though it is also true that his conception of the feminine being is anything but traditional and that it bears no resemblance to the conventional picture of the woman as wife/mother.

9   I have been unable to identify any claim that Levinas makes to that effect. However, his description of the feminine in *Totality and Infinity* and *Time and the Other* certainly makes it seem as if he had said that. See also Chanter, 2005.

10 Following Hölderlin, Heidegger also describes the home at one point as an 'asylum' in his lecture on *Der Ister* (see *HH* 20).

11 The question remains: Who or what welcomes feminine alterity? Having no determinable identity, feminine alterity would be welcomed under the terms of an unconditional hospitality. But the subject that would welcome feminine alterity in that way would also have to be without a determinable identity (as subject, self, ego, consciousness, etc.).

Chapter 4

1   I do not distinguish between what Hölderlin means when he writes something in a poem or letter and what Heidegger takes him to mean, unless it is necessary, as in section 6 where I distinguish between the standard reading of Hölderlin on the relation between the foreign and the proper and Heidegger's unusual interpretation of it.

2   This talk of the look is reminiscent of Derrida's (1994: 7) talk of the *visor effect* in *Spectres of Marx*: to 'feel ourselves seen by a look which it will always be impossible to cross'.

3 Is this a thinking of the homeland beyond nationalism or the identity of the nation?

4 See de Beistegui (1998: 128–45) and Strong (2018) for an interpretation of Heidegger's reading of this expression.

5 Heidegger draws this polemical logic of appearing from Heraclitus's Fragment 53: 'War is the father of all and king of all; and some he has made gods and some men, some bond and some free.' He sees that logic at work in Hölderlin's notion of nature or the holy.

6 Kearney's explanation of this phenomenon is different than the one proposed here. On his account, the stranger incarnates the monstrous or divine owing to our fractured psyche. Instead of acknowledging that there is an inner alterity that haunts us, we repudiate it by projecting it onto others (Kearney, 2003: 4). That psychological account seems to me to be insufficient, since what calls for an explanation is the strangeness of the other, not the inner strangeness of the self. The former, as I argued in Chapter 2, is not reducible to the latter.

7 The blowing of the northeasterly wind in *Andenken* can be read both ways, as the greeting sent by the foreigner from the Orient to the Hesperian poet or as the poet's remembrance of the same. That greeting, or its remembrance, sets the Hesperian poet on his journey home.

Chapter 5

1 A version of this chapter appeared in *Journal of the British Society for Phenomenology* Vol. 44 (3) under the title 'Nietzsche and Heidegger: ethics beyond metaphysics.' I thank the editor, Ulli Haase, for permission to use it.

2 For example, Aquinas explains that truth is primarily in the intellect and secondarily in the thing: in the former, because the conformity of the intellect to the thing cannot be expressed anywhere but in the intellect; in the latter, because the thing has a quality or form that makes it adequate to the intellect in the sense that it causes knowledge of itself by means of its species received in the soul (Aquinas, 1998: 171, 178, 185). Let me add that both Aristotle and Aquinas offer non-propositional accounts of truth as well. Aristotle (2014) speaks of the truth of non-composite essences at the end of *Metaphysics* IX.1051b24-25, which are made available in an intuition rather than in a judgment. So also for Aquinas: truth is known by the divine intellect intuitively not in a judgment.

3 Heidegger insists in the *Parmenides* lecture that Luther is the first to connect truth with justice: 'Luther asks how man could be a "true" Christian, that is, a just man, a man fit for what is just, a justified man' (51). Truth here becomes a matter of justice. See also Bret Davis (2007: 166).

4 Tracy Colony (2011: 207) suggests that the formulation of the will to power as the essence and the eternal return as the existence of the world in the 1936–7 courses on art and the eternal return is a late editorial addition of Heidegger's.

5 Although I cannot explore this here, Heidegger contends in section 110 of his *Contributions to Philosophy (from the Event)* that there is in fact no discontinuity between modern idealism and the emerging naturalism of the mid-nineteenth century, as they are both offshoots of Platonism (see *CP* 173). I am thankful to Dan Dahlstrom for pointing this out to me.

6 Is there a connection between the understanding of being as subjectivity and the twofold legacy of the Enlightenment, as Frederick Beiser (2000) describes it, namely scientific naturalism and rational criticism, and the so-called crisis of the Enlightenment that it brought about, that is, scientific materialism and scepticism?

7 Alain de Libera (2007: 98–101) argues that the *I* doesn't become part of everyday philosophical discourse before Locke's *Essay*, in particular, in the moral-juridical context that deals with the imputation of responsibility to the self.

8 If I am not anxious or distressed about what *being* signifies then that is tantamount to saying that I take for granted (a) the appearing of entities in the world and (b) how I live my existence in the world.

9 Tom Stern contends that 'what Nietzsche wants us to learn to love and make beautiful is the error that conditions our existence [. . .] What he recommends is the artistic appropriation of these errors at a second-order level – to make these errors beautiful' (Stern, 2013: 9–10). Nietzsche does say in a brief parenthesis in the *Genealogy* that art is the only antidote to the ascetic ideal – 'art, in which precisely the lie is sanctioned and the will to deception has a good conscience' (Nietzsche, 1989: 153). But there are indications in the text that suggest that Nietzsche may not think that art is a sufficient response to nihilism and the ascetic ideal (why does he allude to it only parenthetically?), and that what is required in addition is an *ethical* appropriation of these errors, that is, an appropriation of them as obstacles to the way we ordinarily understand ourselves and in relation to which we are to test the strength of our character or will.

10 Nietzsche is close to Hegel's *Phenomenology of Spirit* in that regard in which the trajectory of ordinary consciousness is described as a pathway of doubt and despair. When I commit myself to the truth of *p*, I stake my being on it. So when I become conscious of its untruth, I lose my sense of self as well.

11 Laurence Hatab and Christa Davis Acampara have argued that the sovereign individual does not function as a positive exemplar for Nietzsche. I am not convinced by their argument. Acampara contends that the standard view cannot be supported because 'reference to such a being is limited to the one section under consideration', that is, GM II 2, and because it commits Nietzsche to certain ideas about subjectivity that he rejects, such as the distinction between

the doer and the deed (Acampara, 2006: 152–3). Hatab's point is roughly the same: '[t]he sovereign individual names ... the modern ideal of subjective autonomy, which Nietzsche *rejects*' (Hatab, 2005: 54). Acampara's first claim is incorrect. Nietzsche emphasizes the importance of learning to keep one's word on two other occasions in his late notebooks, which I cite above. Second, as I read Nietzsche, being able to stand security for one's word, aside from being a test of one's strength and character, is an achievement: it is achieved by overcoming internal resistances, such as the power to forget. In that sense, it exemplifies the *Nietzschean notion of freedom* rather than the modern idea of autonomy as self-determination. Both authors seem to assume that Nietzsche has one ideal type under which all his descriptions of what is *übermenschlich* has to fit. But it is not clear that this is true.

12 Nietzsche provides further examples in *Twilight of the Idols* of what this training and exercise of the will involves. In order to see well, for instance, we must learn to defer judgment: 'not to react immediately to a stimulus, but to have the restraining, stock-tacking instincts in one's control'. The incapacity to resist a stimulus, the need to react and obey every impulse, is a sign of 'decline' and 'symptom of exhaustion' (Nietzsche, 1990: 76). We must submit to these kinds of exercises to have our volitional and cognitive resources under our control.

Chapter 6

1 The translator of Aristotle (1994: 43) notes that *substance* is a conventional yet misleading term for *ousia*, a view shared by many authors such as Aubenque, 2000; Loux, 1991; Wedin, 2002 and Witt, 1989.

2 See Arpe, 1941; Bos, 2000; Braun, 1977; Courtine, 2003; de Ghellinck, 1941 and 1942; Gilson, 2000. We find the following entry in *The Oxford Dictionary of English Etymology*: 'Substance: essence XIII (*Cursor M.*); a being; (philos.) that which underlies phenomena; material, matter; means, wealth XIV. (O)F *substance*, corr. to Pr. *sustancia*, Sp. *sustancia*, It. *sostanza* – post-Augustan L. *substantia* being, essence, material property (formally rendering Gr. *hupostasis*, but used also for *ousia*), f. *substare*, f. *sub* SUB- + *stare* STAND. So substanti*al* XIV – (O)F *substantiel* or Chr. L. *substantialis*, tr. Gr. *hupostatikos*.'

3 Boethius (1997: III.91–5): we 'say that there is one *ousia* or *ousiosis*, that is, one *essentia* or *subsistentia* of the Godhead, but three *upostaseis*, that is three *substantias*. And indeed, following this use, men have spoken of one essence of the trinity (*unam trinitatis essentiam*), three *substantias* and three *personas*. For did not the language of the Church forbid us to say that there are three *substantias* in God?' See Augustine (1963: VII.3.11).

4   In fragment 100 of the *testimonia* on Posidonius (1988), Lucan writes: 'For
    Posidonius, the Stoic, says, "God is intelligent *spiritus* pervading the whole
    materiam [= *ousias*]."' In his translation of Plato's (1975) *Timaeus*, Calcidius
    renders *ousia* once by *divitiae* (11.11), twice by *essentia* (22.8, 29.9) and six times by
    substantia (27.8, 9, 15, 17, 29.11, 51.2). Braun (1977) remarks that Tertullian rejects
    the word *essentia* for the being of the divine (167), that *substantia* presents itself as
    the normal and natural equivalent of *ousia* (179) and that he defines *substantia* as
    the body (*corpus*) of each *res* (81).

5   Mansfield (1992: 90): 'It may safely be assumed that the artificial and to some extent
    superficial harmonizing of Plato, Aristotle and the Stoics ... is not Seneca's doing,
    but stems from the early Middle Platonist tradition(s) on which he depends.' This
    so-called agreement between Plato, Aristotle and the Stoics is often expressed by
    Cicero (1994: IV.1.2; 22.61; 1956, I.1.2).

6   This division of being echoes Plato's passage in the *Sophist* on the *gigantomachia
    peri tes ousias* (2002: 246a3–c4). The Friends of the Forms identify *ousia* with the
    incorporeal, whereas the Sons of the Earth identify it with the corporeal. Plato
    of course does not say that *ousia* is a genus divisible into the corporeal and the
    incorporeal.

7   Note that Seneca presents an unusual Stoic doctrine in this passage. Instead of
    placing the standard incorporeals in the class of non-existent entities – time, place,
    void and meaning – he has fictitious entities.

8   Arpe (1941: 66), Braun (1977: 172) and Courtine (2003: 56) maintain that it is
    meant to replicate the Stoic opposition between *upostasis* and *emphasis*. But it is
    difficult to maintain that thesis with much confidence. The latter opposition is
    fairly unstable and equivocal in Stoicism. *Upostasis* has at least two different senses
    in Stoicism: (a) for the Posidonian school, the term signifies a body as opposed to
    an appearance; (b) but for the earlier Stoics, the term is contrasted precisely with
    ousia = body, and is reserved for the incorporeals. See Goldschmidt (1972: 331–45).

9   Rutledge (2007: 109–21) stresses the importance of rhetoric during the
    Imperial Age.

10 Cicero (1960: 5.23): 'Whether its subject is the nature of the heavens or of the earth,
    the power of gods or men ...'

11 Quintilian (1924: II.21.13): 'philosophers only usurped this department of
    knowledge [i.e. on the honorable, the good, the just and the expedient] after it had
    been abandoned by the orators: it was always the peculiar property of rhetoric
    and the philosophers are really trespassers'. Quintilian adds that since dialectic is a
    concise form of oratory, whatever is brought before the dialectician or philosopher
    should *a fortiori* be regarded as also appropriate for oratory.

12 Veyne (1997: 171): 'Roman epitaphs reflected not some fundamental idea of death
    but the reign of public rhetoric.'

13 Quintilian (1924: III.6.21) reports Hermagoras's definition of stasis: 'a *status* is that which enables the subject [= conflict] to be understood and to which the proofs of the parties concerned will also be directed'.

14 Quintilian (1924: III.6.80): 'there are three things on which enquiry is made in every case: we ask whether a thing is, what it is, and of what kind it is (*quod, quid sit et quale sit*). Nature herself imposes this upon us. For, first of all, there must be some being (*subesse aliquid*) for the question, since we cannot possibly determine what a thing is, or of what kind it is, until we have first ascertained whether it is, and therefore the first question raised is whether it is.'

15 See Bos (2000: 511–37) for the empirico-nominalistic reading of Aristotle's *Categories* in the pseudo-Augustinian *Paraphrasis Themistiana*, and Courtine (2003: 16–33) for the same in Boethius' commentary on Aristotle's text.

Bibliography

Acampara, Christa Davis. 2006. 'On Sovereignty and Overhumanity: Why It Matters How We Read Nietzsche's Genealogy II: 2'. In *Nietzsche's On the Genealogy of Morals: Critical Essays*. Ed. Christa Davis Acampara. Lanham and Oxford: Rowman & Littlefield.

Ansell Pearson, Keith, and Large, Duncan. 2006. *The Nietzsche Reader*. Malden, MA, Oxford, Carlton and Victoria: Blackwell Publishing.

Apollinaris, Sidonius. 1963. *Poems and Letters*. Trans. W. B. Anderson, Cambridge, MA and London: Harvard University Press.

Apuleius. 1997. *The Metamorphosis or Golden Ass and Philosophical Works of Apuleius*. Trans. T. Taylor, London: Kessinger Publishing.

Aquinas, Thomas. 1998. *Selected Writings*. Trans. Ralph Mcinerny, London: Penguin Books.

Aristotle. *Metaphysics Z and H*. 1994. Trans. David Bostock, Oxford: Clarendon Press.

Aristotle. 2000. *The Complete Works Vol. 1 and Vol.2*. Ed. Jonathan Barnes. Princeton: Princeton University Press.

Aristotle. 2014. *Metaphysics, Volume I: Books 1-9*. Trans. Hugh Tredennick, Cambridge, MA: Harvard University Press.

Arpe, Curt. 1941. 'Substantia', *Philologus* 94: 65–78.

Aubenque, Pierre. 2000. 'Sur l'ambivalence du concept Aristotélicien de substance'. In *Ontologie et dialogue: Mélanges en hommage à Pierre Aubenque*. Ed. N. L. Cordero, 373–89. Paris: Vrin.

Augustine. 1963. *The Trinity*. Trans. S. McKenna, Washington, DC: Catholic University of America Press.

Babich, Babette. 2014. 'Constellating Technology: Heidegger's Die Gefahr/The Danger'. In *The Multidimensionality of Hermeneutic Phenomenology*. Ed. Babette Babich and Dimitri Ginev, 153–82. Frankfurt am Main: Springer.

Bambach, Charles. 1995. *Heidegger, Dilthey, and the Crisis of Historicism*. Ithaca, NY: Cornell University Press.

Barilli, Renato. 1989. *Rhetoric*. Trans. G. Menozzi, *Theory and History of Literature, Vol. 63*. Minneapolis: University of Minnesota Press.

Beiser, Frederick. 2000. 'The Enlightenment and Idealism'. In *The Cambridge Companion to German Idealism*. Ed. Karl Ameriks. Cambridge: Cambridge University Press.

Bernasconi, Robert. 2005. 'Levinas and the Struggle for Existence'. In *Addressing Levinas*. Ed. Eric Sean Nelson, Antje Kapust and Kent Still, 170–85. Evanston, IL: Northwestern University Press.

Bernasconi, Robert, and Wood, David, eds. 2003. *The Provocation of Levinas: Rethinking the Other*. London and New York: Routledge.

Blanchot, Maurice. 1982. *The Space of Literature*. Trans. Ann Smock, Lincoln and London: University of Nebraska Press.

Boethius. 1997. 'Contra Eutychen'. In *The Theological Tractates*. Trans. H. F. Stewart, E. K. Rand and S. J. Tester. *The Consolation of Philosophy*. Trans. S. J. Tester, 2–128. Cambridge, MA and London: Harvard University Press.

Bos, Egbert. 2000. 'Some Notes on the Meaning of the Term *"Substantia"* in the Tradition of Aristotle's Aristotle's Categories'. In *L'élaboration du vocabulaire philosophique au moyen âge*. Ed. J. Hamesse and C. Steel, 511–39. Turnhout: Brepols.

Brassier, Ray. 2007. *Nihil Unbound: Enlightenment and Extinction*. London and New York: Palgrave Macmillan.

Braun, René. 1977. *Deus christianorum. Recherches sur le vocabulaire doctrinal de Tertullien*. Paris: Études Augustiniennes.

Butler, Judith. 1990. *Gender Trouble: Feminism and the Subversion of Identity*. New York and London: Routledge.

Butler, Judith. 2009. *Frames of War: When Is Life Grievable?* London and New York: Verso.

Carman, Taylor. 2005. 'Authenticity'. In *A Companion to Heidegger*. Ed. Hubert L. Dreyfus and Mark A. Wrathall. Oxford: Blackwell Publishing.

Carr, David. 1999. *The Paradox of Subjectivity: The Self in the Transcendental Tradition*. Oxford: Oxford University Press.

Casey S., Edward. 2011 'Strangers at the Edge of Hospitality'. In *Phenomenologies of the Stranger: Between Hostility and Hospitality*. Ed. Richard Kearney and Kascha Semonovitch. New York: Fordham University Press.

Chanter, Tina. 2003. 'Feminism and the Other'. In *The Provocation of Levinas: Rethinking the Other*. Ed. Robert Bernasconi and David Wood. London and New York: Routledge.

Chanter, Tina. 2005. 'Conditions: The Politics of Ontology and the Temporality of the Feminine'. In *Addressing Levinas*. Ed. Eric Sean Nelson, Antje Kapust and Kent Still. Evanston, IL: Northwestern University Press.

Cicero, Marcus Tullius. 1928. *De Officiis*. Trans. Walter Miller, London and New York: G. P. Putnam's Sons.

Cicero, Marcus Tullius. 1935. *De natura deorum, Academica*. Trans. H. Rackham, London: Heinemann.

Cicero, Marcus Tullius. 1960. *De oratore Book III, Together with De fato, Paradoxa stoicorum, De partitione oratoria*. Trans. H. Rackham, Cambridge, MA and London: Harvard University Press.

Cicero, Marcus Tullius. 1994. *De finibus bonorum et malorum*. Trans. H. Rackham, Cambridge, MA and London: Harvard University Press.

Cicero, Marcus Tullius. 2001. *Tusculan disputations*. Trans. J. E. King, Cambridge, MA and London: Harvard University Press.

Cicero, Marcus Tullius. 2003. *Topica*. Trans. T. Reinhardt, Oxford: Oxford University Press.

Clark, Maudemarie. 1991. *Nietzsche on Truth and Philosophy*. Cambridge: Cambridge University Press.

Cohen, Richard A. 2006. 'Levinas: Thinking Least about Death–Contra Heidegger'. In *International Journal for Philosophy of Religion* 60: 21–39.

Colony, Tracy. 2011. 'The Death of God and the Life of Being: Heidegger's Confrontation with Nietzsche'. In *Interpreting Heidegger: Critical Essays*. Ed. Daniel O. Dahlstrom, Cambridge: Cambridge University Press.

Courtine, Jean-François. 1991. 'Voice of Conscience and Call of Being'. In *Who Comes after the Subject?* Ed. Eduardo Cadava, Peter Connor and Jean-Luc Nancy, New York and London: Routledge.

Courtine, Jean-François. 2003. 'Les traduction latines d'OUSIA et la comprehension romano-stoïcienne de l'être'. In *Les catégories de l'être*, 11–77. Paris: PUF.

Crowe, Benjamin D. 2007. 'Heidegger's Gods'. In *International Journal of Philosophical Studies* 15, no. 2: 225–45.

Crowell, Steven Galt. 2001. *Husserl, Heidegger, and the Space of Meaning: Paths toward Transcendental Phenomenology*. Evanston, IL: Northwestern University Press.

Dastur, Françoise. 2002. 'The Call of Conscience: The Most Intimate Alterity'. In *Heidegger and Practical Philosophy*. Ed. François Raffoul and David Pettigrew, Albany: State University of New York Press.

Davis, Bret. 2007. *Heidegger and the Will: On the Way to Gelassenheit*. Evanston, IL: Northwestern University Press.

de Beistegui, Miguel. 1998. *Heidegger & the Political: Dystopias*. London and New York: Routledge.

de Ghellinck, Jean. 1941. 'L'entrée d'essentia, substantia, et autres mots apparentés, dans le latin médiéval.' In *Archivum Latinatis Medii Aevi* 16: 77–112.

de Ghellinck, Jean. 1942. 'Essentia et substantia. Note complémentaire'. In *Archivum Latinatis Medii Aevi* 17: 129–133.

de Libera, Alain. 2007. *Archéologie du sujet. I. Naissance du sujet*. Paris: Vrin.

de Man, Paul. 1996. *Aesthetic Ideology Theory and History of Literature Volume 65*. Minneapolis, London: University of Minnesota Press.

de Man, Paul. 2012. 'Hölderlin and the Romantic Tradition'. In *Diacritics* 40, no. 1: 100–29.

Derrida, Jacques. 1979. *Spurs: Nietzsche's Styles*. Trans. Barbara Harlow, Chicago, IL and London: Chicago University Press.

Derrida, Jacques. 1982. 'White Mythology: Metaphor in the Text of Philosophy'. In *Margins of Philosophy*. Trans. Alan Bass, Sussex: The Harvester Press.

Derrida, Jacques. 1985. *Otobiographies: The Teaching of Nietzsche and the Politics of the Proper Name*. Trans. Avital Ronnell, New York: Schocken Books.

Derrida, Jacques. 1989. *Memoires for Paul de Man*. Trans. Cecile Lindsay, Jonathan Culler, Eduardo Cadava and Peggy Kamuf, New York: Columbia University Press.

Derrida, Jacques. 1991. '"Eating Well," or the Calculation of the Subject: An Interview with Jacques Derrida'. In *Who Comes after the Subject?* Ed. Eduardo Cadava, Peter Connor and Jean-Luc Nancy. New York and London: Routledge.

Derrida, Jacques. 1993. *Aporias*. Trans. Thomas Dutoit, Stanford, CA: Stanford University Press.

Derrida, Jacques. 1994. *Specters of Marx: The State of the Debt, the Work of Mourning and the New International*. Trans. Peggy Kamuf, New York and London: Routledge.

Derrida, Jacques. 1996. *The Gift of Death*. Trans. David Wills, Chicago, IL, London: Chicago University Press.

Derrida, Jacques. 1999. 'Hospitality, Justice and Responsibility: A Dialogue with Jacques Derrida'. In *Questioning Ethics: Contemporary Debates in Philosophy*. Ed. Richard Kearney and Mark Dooley, London and New York: Routledge.

Derrida, Jacques. 2000. 'Hostipitality'. *Angelaki: Journal of the Theoretical Humanities* 5, no. 3: 3–18.

Derrida, Jacques. 2000a. *Of Hospitality*. Trans. Rachel Bowlby, Stanford, CA: Stanford University Press.

Derrida, Jacques. 2001. *A Taste for the Secret*. Trans. Giacomo Donis, Cambridge, UK: Polity.

Derrida, Jacques. 2001a. *Writing and Difference*. Trans. Alan Bass, London and New York: Routledge.

Derrida, Jacques. 2007. 'A Certain Impossible Possibility of Saying the Event'. In *Critical Inquiry* 33, no. 2.

Derrida, Jacques. 2008. *The Animal That Therefore I Am*. Trans. David Willis, New York: Fordham University Press.

Dreyfus, Hubert L. 1972. *What Computers Can't do: A Critique of Artificial Reason*. New York, Evanston, San Francisco, London: Harper & Row.

Edkins, Jenny. 2007. 'Whatever Politics'. In *Giorgio Agamben: Sovereignty & Life*. Ed. Matthew Calarco and Steven DeCaroli. Stanford, CA: Stanford University Press

Fink, Eugen. 1995. *Sixth Cartesian Meditation: The Idea of a Transcendental Theory of Method*. Trans. Ronald Buzina, Bloomington and Indianapolis: Indiana University Press.

Foucault, Michel. 2002. *The Order of Things: An Archeology of the Human Sciences*. London and New York: Routledge.

Frontinus. 1925. *The Stratagems: The Aqueducts of Rome*. Trans. C. E. Bennett, Cambridge, MA: Harvard University Press.

Gaius. 1988. *The Institutes of Gaius*. Trans. W. M. Gordon and O. F. Robinson, with the Latin text of Seckel & Kuebler. London: Duckworth.

Gilson, E. 2000. *L'Être et l'essence*. Paris: Vrin.

Goldschmidt, Victor. 1972. '"Uparchein" et "uphistanai" dans la philosophie stoïcienne'. In *Revue des études Grecques* 2: 331–45.

Greisch, Jean. 2005. 'Ethics and Ontology: Some Hypocritical Reflections'. In *Emmanuel Levinas: Critical Assessments of Leading Philosophers*. Ed. Claire Katz and Lara Trout, 215–27. *Volume I: Levinas, Phenomenology and His Critics*. London and New York: Routledge.

Hadot, Pierre. 1968. *Porphyre et Victorinus*. Paris: Études Augustiniennes.

Hatab, Lawrence J. 2005. *Nietzsche's Life Sentence: Coming to Terms with Eternal Recurrence*. London and New York: Routledge.

Havas, Randall. 1995. *Nietzsche's Genealogy, Nihilism and the Will to Knowledge*. Ithaca, NY and London: Cornell University Press.

Hegel, G. W. F. 1977. *Hegel's Phenomenology of Spirit*. Trans. A. V. Miller. Oxford, New York, Toronto and Melbourne: Oxford University Press.

Henrich, Dieter. 1997. *The Course of Remembrance and Other Essays*. Stanford, CA: Stanford University Press.

Hölderlin, Friedrich. 1988. *Essays and Letters on Theory*. Trans. Thomas Pfau, Albany: State University of New York Press.

Hölderlin, Friedrich. 2011. *Hyperion*. Trans. Ross Benjamin, Brooklyn, NY: Archipelago Books.

Kearney, Richard, 1986. Ed. *Face to Face with Levinas*. Albany: State University of New York.

Kearney, Richard. 2003. *Strangers, Gods and Monsters: Interpreting Otherness*. London and New York: Routledge.

Kisiel, Theodore. 1995. *The Genesis of Heidegger's Being and Time*. Berkeley, Los Angeles and London: University of California Press.

Krell, David Farrell. 1992. *Daimon Life: Heidegger and Life-Philosophy*. Bloomington and Indianapolis: Indiana University Press.

Lacoue-Labarthe, Philippe. 1989. *Typography: Mimesis, Philosophy, Politics*. London, England and Cambridge, MA: Harvard University Press.

Lafont, Cristina. 2000. *Heidegger, Language, and World-Disclosure*. Trans. Graham Harman, Cambridge: Cambridge University Press.

Laing, Ronald David. 1969. *The Divided Self: An Existential Study in Sanity and Madness*. London: Penguin Books.

Levinas, Emmanuel. 1979. *Totality and Infinity: An Essay on Exteriority*. Trans. Alphonso Lingis, The Hague, Boston and London: Martinus Nijhoff.

Levinas, Emmanuel. 1987. *Time and the Other (and Additional Essays)*. Trans. Richard A. Cohen, Pittsburgh, PA: Duquesne University Press.

Levinas, Emmanuel. 1987a. *Collected Philosophical Papers*. Trans. Alphonso Lingis, Dordrecht, Boston and Lancaster: Martinus Nijhoff.

Levinas, Emmanuel. 1998. *On Thinking-of-the-Other: Entre Nous*. Trans. Michael B. Smith and Barbara Harshav, New York: Columbia University Press.

Levinas, Emmanuel. 1990. *Difficult Freedom: Essays on Judaism*. Trans. Seán Hand. Baltimore, MD: John Hopkins University Press.

Levinas, Emmanuel. 1997. *Difficult Freedom*. Trans. Seán Hand, Baltimore, MD: Johns Hopkins University Press.

Lingis, Alphonso. 1994. *The Community of Those Who Have Nothing in Common*. Bloomington and Indianapolis: Indiana University Press.

Llewelyn, John. 1995. *Emmanuel Levinas: The Genealogy of Ethics*. London and
New York: Routledge.

Loux, Michael. 1991. *Primary Ousia: An Essay on Aristotle's Metaphysics Zeta and Eta*.
Ithaca, NY: Cornell University Press.

Lyotard, Jean-François. 1997. *Heidegger and 'the jews'*. Trans. Andreas Michel and Mark
S. Roberts, Minneapolis and London: University of Minnesota Press.

Mansfield, Jaap. 1992. *Heresiography in Context: Hipolytus' Elenchos as a Source for
Greek Philosophy*. Leiden, New York and Köln: E. J. Brill.

Meillassoux, Quentin. 2008. *After Finitude: An Essay on the Necessity of Contingency*.
Trans. Ray Brassier, London and New York: Bloomsbury.

Mortley, Raoul. 1991. *French Philosophers in Conversation*. New York and
London: Routledge.

Nietzsche, Friedrich. 1968. *The Will to Power*. Trans. Walter Kaufmann and R. J.
Hollingdale. New York: Vintage Books.

Nietzsche, Friedrich. 1989. *On the Genealogy of Morals*. Trans. Walter Kaufmann and R.
J. Hollingdale, *Ecce Homo*. Trans. Walter Kaufmann. New York: Vintage Books.

Nietzsche, Friedrich. 1990. *Twilight of the Idols and Anti-Christ*. Trans. R. J. Hollingdale,
London: Penguin Books.

Nietzsche, Friedrich. 1997. *Untimely Meditations*. Ed. Daniel Breazeale, Cambridge:
Cambridge University Press.

Nietzsche, Friedrich. 2003. Writings *from the Late Notebooks*. Cambridge: Cambridge
University Press.

Nietzsche, Friedrich. 2008. *The Gay Science with a Prelude in German Rhymes
and an Appendix of Songs*. Trans. Josefine Nauckhoff, Cambridge: Cambridge
University Press.

Of Cusa, Nicholas. 1973. *Nicholas of Cusa on God as Not-Other*. Trans. Jasper Hopkins,
Minneapolis: University of Minnesota Press.

Oudemans, Wouter, and Lardinois, Andre. 1987. *Tragic Ambiguity: Anthropology,
Philosophy and Sophocles' Antigone*. Leiden, New York, København and Köln: E.
J. Brill.

Perpich, Diane. 2001. 'From the Caress to the Word: Transcendence and the Feminine
in the Philosophy of Emmanuel Levinas'. In *Feminist Interpretations of Emmanuel
Levinas*. Ed. Tina Chanter. University Park: Pennsylvania State University Press.

Perpich, Diane. 2010. 'Levinas, Feminism, and Identity Politics'. In *Radicalizing
Levinas*. Ed. Peter Atterton and Matthew Calarco. Albany: State University of
New York Press.

Plato. 1975. *Latinus*. Vol. 4. *Timaeus*. Londinii: in aedibus Instituti Warburgiani.

Plato. 2002. *Sophist*. Trans. H. N. Fowler, Cambridge, MA and London: Harvard
University Press.

Posidonius. 1988. *Posidonius*. Ed. I. G. Kidd, Vol. 1. Cambridge: Cambridge
University Press.

Pseudo-Quintilian. 1982. *Declamationes XIX maiores*. Ed. Lennart Hakanson, Stutgardiae: Teubner.

Quintilian. 1924. *Institutionis oratoriae*. Ed. F. H. Colson, Cambridge: Cambridge University Press.

Raffoul, François. 2005. 'Being and the Other: Ethics and Ontology in Levinas and Heidegger'. In *Addressing Levinas*. Ed. Eric Sean Nelson, Antje Kapust and Kent Still. Evanston, IL: Northwestern University Press.

Raffoul, François. 2010. *The Origins of Responsibility*. Bloomington and Indianapolis: Indiana University Press.

Ricoeur, Paul. 1992. *Oneself as Another*. Trans. Kathleen Blamey, Chicago and London: Chicago University Press.

Rutledge, Steven. 2007. 'Oratory and Politics in the Empire'. In *A Companion to Roman Rhetoric*. Ed W. Dominik and J. Hall. Malden, MA and Oxford: Blackwell Publishing.

Schmidt, Dennis J. 2001. *On Germans and Other Greeks: Tragedy and Ethical Life*. Bloomington and Indianapolis: Indiana University Press.

Seneca. 1925. *Ad Lucilium epistulae morales*. Trans. R. M. Gummere, in 3 Volumes, Cambridge, MA and London: Harvard University Press.

Seneca. 1935. *Moral Essays*. Trans. J. W. Basore, Vols I–III. Cambridge, MA and London: Harvard University Press.

Sophocles. 2009. *The Theban Plays: Oedipus the King, Oedipus at Colonus, Antigone*. Trans. Ruth Fainlight and Robert J. Littman, Baltimore, MD: Johns Hopkins University Press.

Stern, Tom. 2013. 'Nietzsche, Amor Fati and The Gay Science'. In *Proceedings of the Aristotelian Society*, Issue 2, Volume CXIII.

Strong, Tracy. 1988. *Friedrich Nietzsche and the Politics of Transfiguration*. Urbana and Chicago: University of Illinois Press.

Strong, Tracy. 2018. 'Heidegger, the *Pólis*, the Political and *Gelassenheit*'. In *Identity and Difference*. Ed. Rafael Winkler, London and New York: Routledge.

Tacitus. 2001. *Dialogus de oratoribus*. Ed. R. Mayor, Cambridge: Cambridge University Press.

Van Buren, John. 1994. *The Young Heidegger: Rumor of the Hidden King*. Bloomington and Indianapolis: Indiana University Press.

Veyne, Paul. 1997. *The Roman Empire*. Trans. A. Goldhammer, Cambridge, MA and London: The Belknap Press of Harvard University Press.

Visker, Rudi. 2004. *The Inhuman Condition: Looking for Difference after Levinas and Heidegger*. New York, Boston, Dordrecht, London and Moscow: Kluwer Academic.

Warminski, Andrzej. 1987. *Reading in Interpretation: Hölderlin, Hegel, Heidegger. Theory and History of Literature, Volume 26*. Minneapolis: University of Minnesota Press.

Wedin, Michael. 2002. *Aristotle's Theory of Substance: The Categories and Metaphysics Zeta*. Oxford: Oxford University Press.

Winkler, Rafael, ed. 2016. *Identity and Difference: Contemporary Debates on the Self.* London and New York: Palgrave Macmillan.

Witt, Charlotte. 1989. *Substance and Essence in Aristotle: An Interpretation of Metaphysics VII-IX.* Ithaca, NY and London: Cornell University Press.

Wood, David. 2005. *The Step Back: Ethics and Politics after Deconstruction.* Albany: State University of New York Press.

Young, Julian. 2002. *Heidegger's Later Philosophy.* Cambridge: Cambridge University Press.

Zahavi, Dan. 1999. *Self-Awareness and Alterity: A Phenomenological Investigation.* Evanston, IL: Northwestern University Press.

Index

CPSIA information can be obtained
at www.ICGtesting.com
Printed in the USA
LVHW10*0751260918
591400LV00008B/65/P